Other Books By Robert M. Barnes

1. *Don't Tread On Me!(Get Outta My Face!)*, Red Lead Press, Pittsburgh, Pa. 2012
2. *Bad Times, Great Markets*, AuthorHouse, Bloomington IN, 2011
3. *Trading Systems Analysis*, McGraw Hill, New York, 1997
4. *Trading In Choppy Markets*, Richard D. Irwin, New York 1997
5. *High Impact Day Trading*,Richard D. Irwin,New York,1996
6. *Cutting Edge Futures Trading Methods For The 21ˢᵗ Century*, Windsor Books, Brightwaters, N.Y. 1996
7. *Megaprofit Commodity Methods*, Windsor Books, Brightwaters, N.Y.,1983
8. *Commodity Portfolio Performance Handbook*, Van Nostrand Reinhold, New York, 1982
9. *Making High Profits In Uncertain Times:Successful Investing In Inflation and Depression*, Van Nostrand Reinhold, New york, 1982
10. *1982 Technical Commodity Yearbook*, Van Nostrand Reinhold, New York,1982
11. *Commodity Profits Through Trend Trading*,John Wiley & Sons, New York, 1982
12. *1981 Commodity Technical Yearbook*, Van Nostrand Reinhold, New york, 1981
13. *Taming The Pits*, John Wiley & Sons, New York,1979
14. *The Dow Theory Can Make You Rich*, Arlington House, New Rochelle, N.Y. 1973

THE BIG
LONG

USING STOPS TO PROFIT MORE AND
REDUCE RISK IN THE LONG-TERM UPTREND

ROBERT BARNES

authorHOUSE

AuthorHouse™
1663 Liberty Drive
Bloomington, IN 47403
www.authorhouse.com
Phone: 833-262-8899

Published by AuthorHouse 10/13/2020

ISBN: 978-1-6655-0395-2 (sc)
ISBN: 978-1-6655-0439-3 (e)

Print information available on the last page.

This book is printed on acid-free paper.

CONTENTS

Figures

Charts

Figure 1 courtesy of Ameritrust
Figure 2 and Charts 3-15 and Table 4(Appendix) courtesy of
Charles Schwab & Co. and Microtrends, a Schwab company.

Tables

The Author can be reached with questions/comments at Rbarnes285@Aol.com

To
Long term investors who want **good** returns with **reasonable** risk
And
Short term traders who desire **large** portfolio returns with **acceptable** risk

INTRODUCTION

Here we go again: bad times, great markets(see my 2011 book, same title). Instead of the economic bubble of 2008-9, caused by economic excesses, no credit, resulting in economic losses(in stocks and in jobs), we have the same malaise and results caused by a COVID virus. Same results, different cause.

Then, it took ten years of rebuilding due to Fed and private actions to regain and sail on to new highs. What will it take now?

Meanwhile, the average investor and indeed institutions were left with the major problem:how to invest to get *reasonable* returns with *acceptable* risk, in all types of markets.

The solution: practical use of *buy and sell stops*, to sharply smooth out losses(by massively decreasing capital drawdowns/strings of losses); and to improve profits: and achieve better portfolio results than the buy-and-hold strategy, for individual stocks and market indicies. (A detailed plan to use stop strategies occurs in Chapter Five).

Long term buy and holders will use the stop methods to reduce risk(*sharply* curtail drawdowns) yet hold onto and *improve* profits; while short terms traders will employ these stop strategies to get *better* profits comparable or better than buy and holders, but also keep portfolio drawdowns(losses) low.

Chapter One explores the long run(thousands of years) of economic and stock activity and concludes that there is *only one trend, the uptrend*, for all of time and especially for the U.S. Market; and hence we should train our investment insights and strategies on a long-term bull market that has long and large relapses, to deal with interim losses but also great investment opportunities.

Chapter Two reviews current and past approaches(from tipsters, pundits, analysts, managers, and funds) to help the investor achieve financial success. A grade of "C" or below is rendered.

Chapter Three presents three important strategies: the venerable buy-and-hold and two better stop strategies for Dow Industrial Average(DIA), S & P 500(SPY) and NASDAQ Composite($COMPX) ETFs; and individual stocks. The theoretical underpinning of these stop strategies is discussed.

Some conclusive tests on these strategies are presented, with caveats on each approach.

Chapter Four tests these three plans on three major indicie ETFs and five or more stocks in each major stock sector for the period 2000-2020. Detailed synopses on many representative stocks are given, overall analysis and tips on the results are presented.

The results in Table 24 for the market indicies ETFs and many sectors' stocks are both *startling* and *spectacular*:both stop strategies show overall *better* return performances and *vastly* improved risk reduction, compared to the buy-and-hold strategy!

Investors and institutions should take note and make major revisions to their investing methodology.

Chapter Five lays out easy, practical plans to implement the three strategies. Anticipated results and prognoses are explained. Discipline and adherence to the plans are strongly recommended and urged. Interest on idle funds and withdrawls are discussed. A *step-by-step* program to use each strategy is set forth.

In Chapter Six, I discuss the crucial aspects of selecting stocks/indicies to invest in, along with future research into improvements to the strategies(different types of buy and sell stops; peak to trough timing, e.g.), along with suggestions of selection of other investment media(options, futures, etc.).

Proper use of stops will help you improve profits, and reduce risk(see Chapter Four).

I strongly believe and hope that this book will help you achieve *and* increase profits and reduce risk.

Savannah, Ga. August 2020

CHAPTER ONE

The Long Term Is Only Up

Really up!

Yes, there will be many retreats, but eventually, always, new highs will be made. Many small retreats(1-2% in size, lasting for days or weeks), a moderate number of bigger drawdowns(5-10% in size), and a few large(25-50%) drops, even a very few unthinkable, unbearable monsters(80-90%) in grand shocks, all lasting from weeks to months, even years.

My initial study of reactions to uptrends(now called drawdowns) in individual stocks(my article 1970 suggested countermoves to uptrends that were well described by an exponential distribution, that were like the ones described above for the general market above: many small ones, a moderate number of average size, and a few big ones(40-50%, even 80-90%, but rarely). Of course, stocks can and have dropped effectively to zero, but I contend the whole market won't, later.

A later study in my book Bad Times, Great Markets(2011) confirmed the same phenomena in the general markets(DJIA) from the 1920s to 2010. It predicted a return to the bull market, at DOW 12,700. The average drawdown was 8.0%, meaning a probability of 5% that retreat of 24% or more could occur in the future. A retreat of 7.2x8.0 or 56% or more has little chance of occurring, about 0.1%. But of course we had 1929, and a 89% drop(a real black swan event). But when, that's the question!

But back to history.

I contend that economic history is made up of a mixture of small and great empires, sometimes contemporary, overlapping and contentious, but a running asset or wealth account of them over time will show a continuous, though sporadic, *uptrend,* despite wars, natural disasters, and human problems.

This admittedly casual analysis starts with ancient civilizations, in chronological, some overlapping, order.

China, India, Japan and middle eastern empires such as Syria, Babylonia, and Persia qualify as the earliest ones that lasted long and had considerable wealth and culture. At almost the same time Egypt and other Mediterranean powers emerged as viable and long lasting empires, followed by Greece, Rome, Carthage and Phoenecia.

Rome was the most clear ruling power until its collapse, which was followed in succession by successful mercantile powers like the Ottoman empire and medieval fiefdoms in Europe. At the end of the middle ages, European powers like England, France, Spain and Germany eventually developed great colonial and industrial empires, followed finally by the United States and other independent nations.

While only recently(200 years ago) did equity exchanges appear, they have grown in importance ever since.

All the empires share similar economic growth attributes: mercantile, trading, asset building capabilities. These are manifested in many ways, from lowly farming to market place to building magnificent structures.

But material progress has had an uneven growth rate. Conflicts and disease alone have taken mighty tolls many times.

It would be difficult to construct business activity across this long time frame, but I think it safe to conclude there has been upwards progress over mankind's existence, albeit uneven and even downwards at times(the middle ages, e.g.). But never to zero! Always some wealth creation at all times.

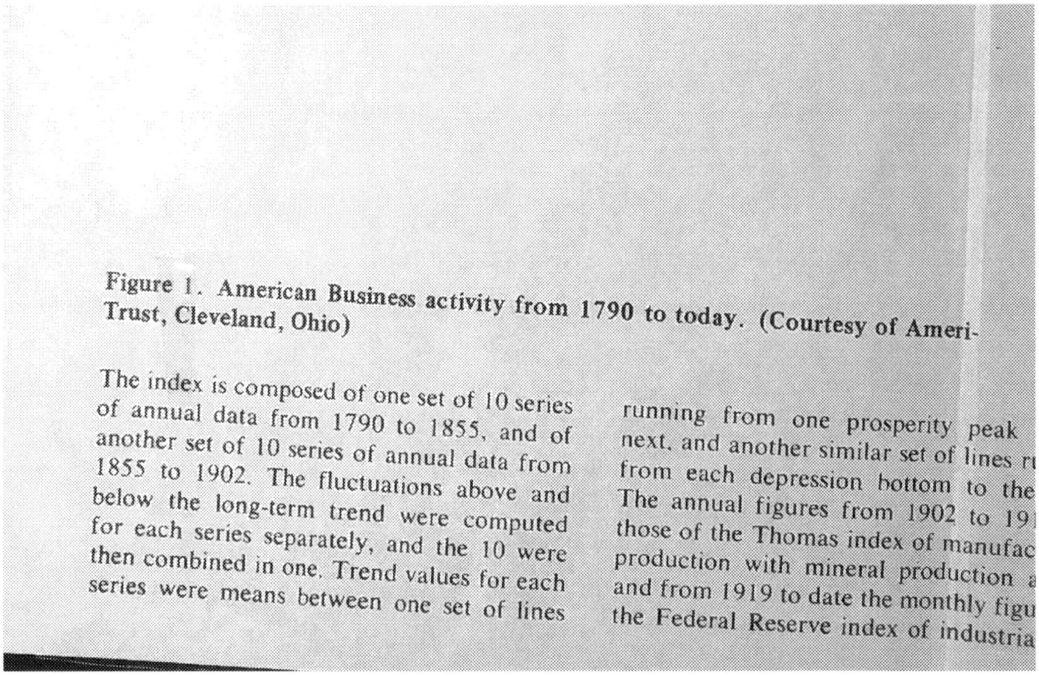

Figure 1. American Business activity from 1790 to today. (Courtesy of Ameri-Trust, Cleveland, Ohio)

The index is composed of one set of 10 series of annual data from 1790 to 1855, and of another set of 10 series of annual data from 1855 to 1902. The fluctuations above and below the long-term trend were computed for each series separately, and the 10 were then combined in one. Trend values for each series were means between one set of lines running from one prosperity peak next, and another similar set of lines r from each depression bottom to the The annual figures from 1902 to 19 those of the Thomas index of manufac production with mineral production a and from 1919 to date the monthly figu the Federal Reserve index of industria

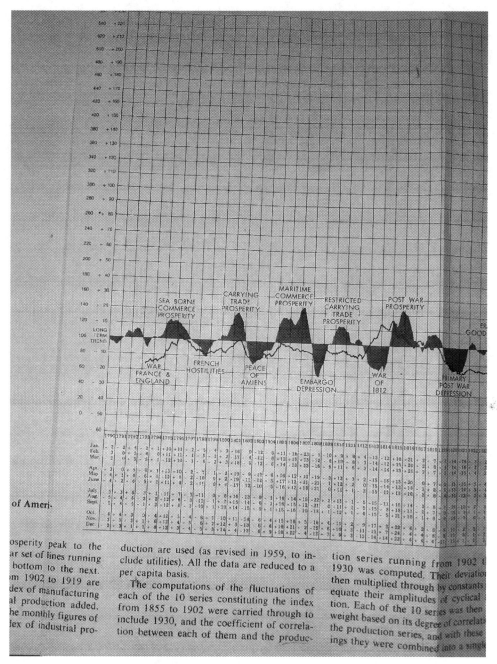

osperity peak to the ar set of lines running bottom to the next. m 1902 to 1919 are dex of manufacturing al production added. he monthly figures of lex of industrial pro-

of Ameri-

duction are used (as revised in 1959, to include utilities). All the data are reduced to a per capita basis.

The computations of the fluctuations of each of the 10 series constituting the index from 1855 to 1902 were carried through to include 1930, and the coefficient of correlation between each of them and the produc-

tion series running from 1902 1930 was computed. Their deviatio then multiplied through by constants equate their amplitudes of cyclical tion. Each of the 10 series was then weight based on its degree of correlat the production series, and with these ings they were combined into a singl

Fig 1 Business Activity 1790-1980

3

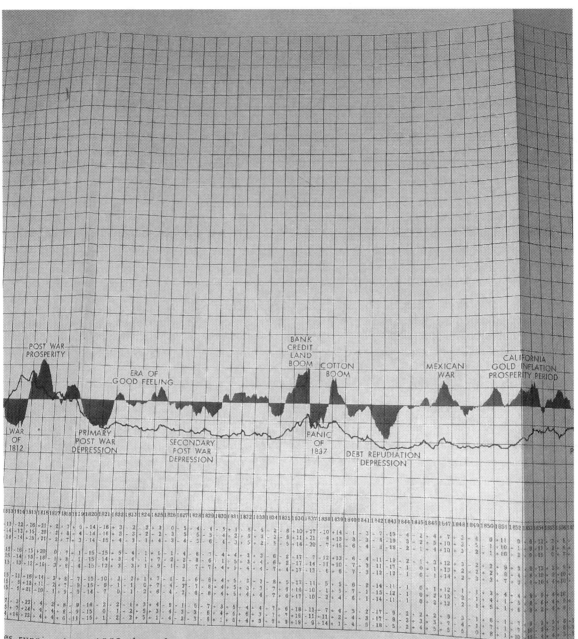

es running from 1902 through computed. Their deviations were plied through by constants so as to ir amplitudes of cyclical fluctua- of the 10 series was then given a ed on its degree of correlation with tion series, and with these weight- were combined into a single index.

The 10 series with these weights are pig iron consumption 15, railroad freight ton miles 15, cotton consumption 14, canal freight (New York and Sault Ste. Marie) 12, coal production 12, construction of miles of new railroads 12, blast furnace activity 10, rail production 6, locomotive production 2, and ship construction 2. The 10 series combined

gave results closely similar production series for the ove 1902 through 1930. The her ties, and the depths of d closely alike in the two se cient of correlation for the Their average deviations for equal.

4

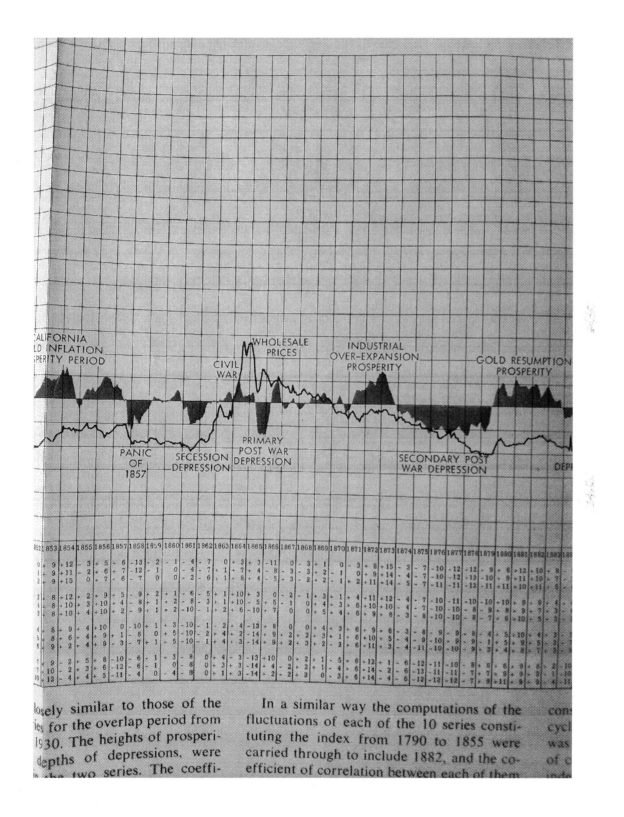

losely similar to those of the
...ies for the overlap period from
...930. The heights of prosperi-
...depths of depressions, were
...the two series. The coeffi-

In a similar way the computations of the
fluctuations of each of the 10 series constituting the index from 1790 to 1855 were
carried through to include 1882, and the coefficient of correlation between each of them

con...
cycl...
was...
of c...
inde...

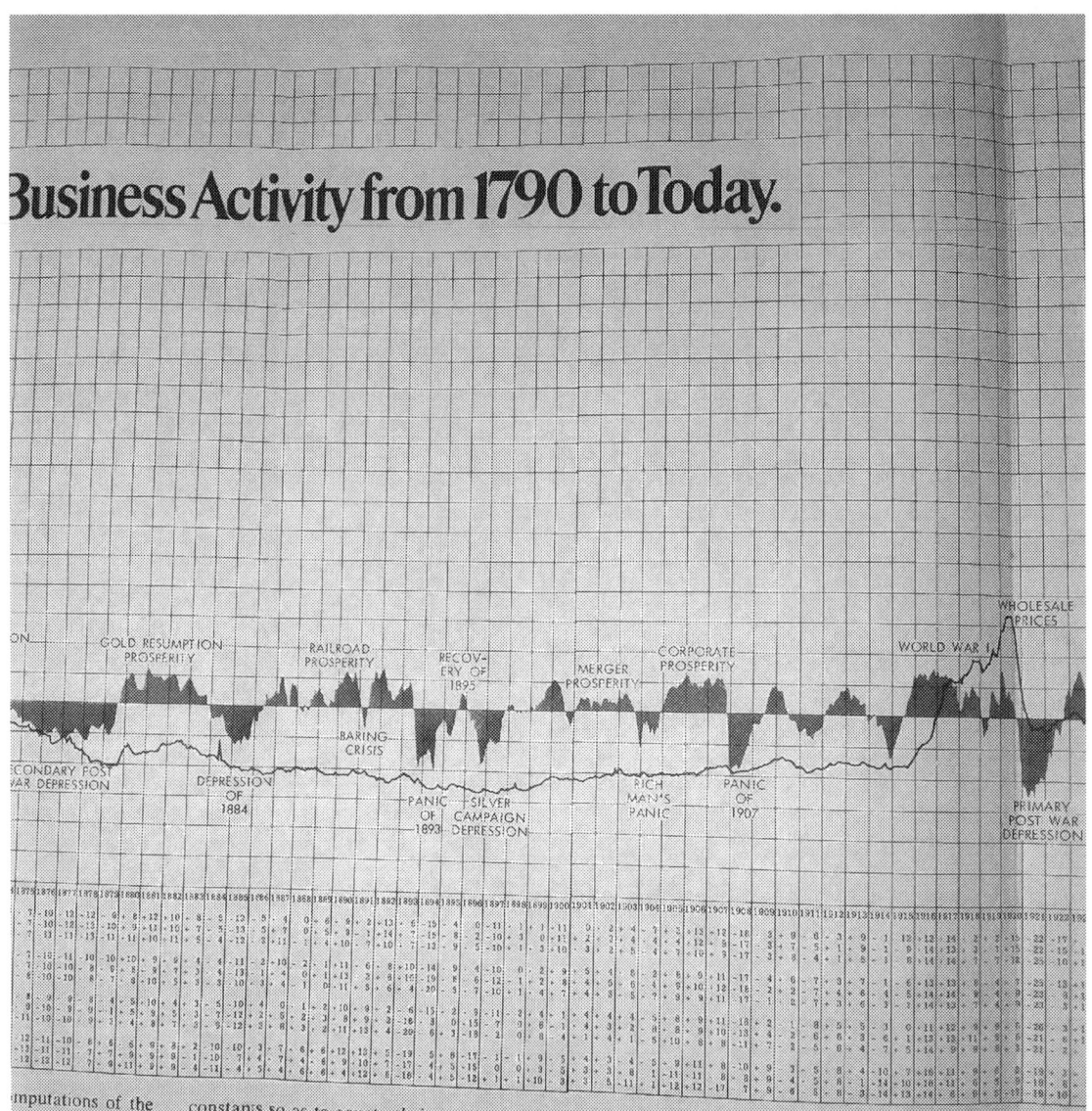

Business Activity from 1790 to Today.

mputations of the
e 10 series consti-
'90 to 1855 were
1882, and the co-
ween each of them
the index running
mputed. Their de-
plied through by

constants so as to equate their amplitudes of cyclical fluctuation. Each of the 10 series was then given a weight based on its degree of correlation with the first 28 years of the index from 1855 to 1902, and with these weightings they were combined into a single index. The 10 series with these weights are commodity prices 20, imports 18, imports

retained for consumption 16, government receipts 14, ship construction 12, government expenditures 6, coal production 6, exports 5, iron exports 2, and tons of registered shipping in service 1. The 10 series combined give results closely similar to those of the other index for the overlap period from 1855 through 1882. The heights of prosperities,

and the
alike in th
relation f
deviations
When
the month
monthly
business

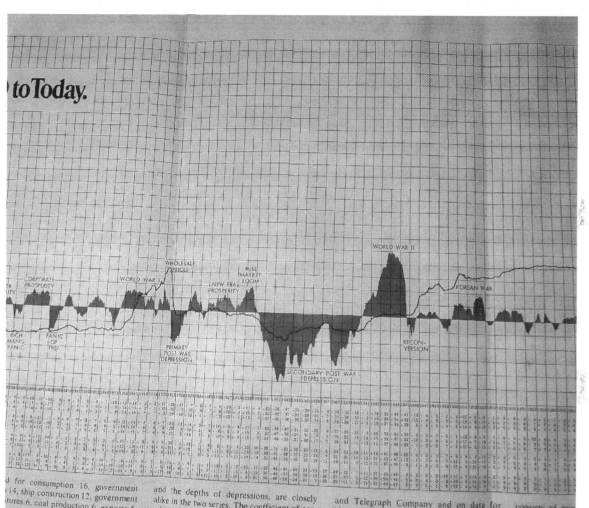

for consumption 16, government
14, ship construction 12, government
itures 6, coal production 6, exports 5,
ports 2, and tons of registered ship-
service 1. The 10 series combined
ults closely similar to those of the
dex for the overlap period from 1855
1882. The heights of prosperities,

and the depths of depressions, are closely
alike in the two series. The coefficient of correlation for the period is .90. Their average
deviations for the period are equal.

When the annual data were determined
the monthly data were fitted to them. These
monthly data were based on the figures of the
business index of the American Telephone

and Telegraph Company and on data for
blast furnace activity from 1877 to 1919.
Monthly data for bank clearings and for
stock prices were used from 1861 to 1877,
and those for security and commodity prices
from 1815 to 1861. From 1790 to 1815 the
monthly data are based on commodity prices.

The long-term trend beginning in 1902

consists of two
method of lea
data. One is us
and the second
was revised in

The black li
wholesale com
(variable weigh

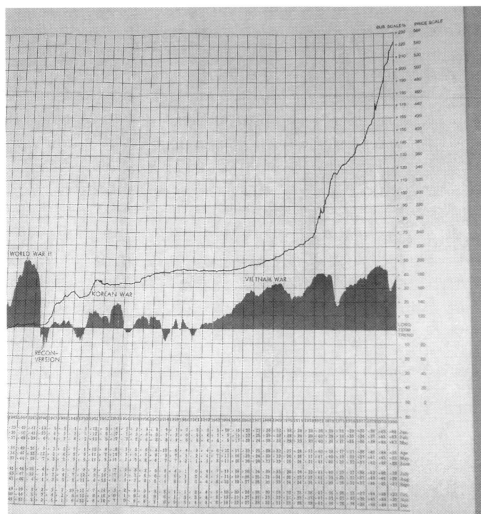

ph Company and on data for
 activity from 1877 to 1919.
 for bank clearings and for
were used from 1861 to 1877,
security and commodity prices
 1861. From 1790 to 1815 the
are based on commodity prices.
rm trend beginning in 1902

consists of two straight lines fitted by the
method of least squares to the per capita
data. One is used from 1902 through 1928
and the second from 1929 to date. The latter
was revised in 1960.

   The black line represents the changes in
wholesale commodity prices. It is the index
(variable weights) of Professors Warren and

Pearson (Cornell), and that of the Bureau of
Labor Statistics, recomputed so that the
average for 1926 equals 100. This series was
used from 1798 to date. From 1795 to 1798
the Stoker series was used.

                    The Fifty-Second Edition, May 1981

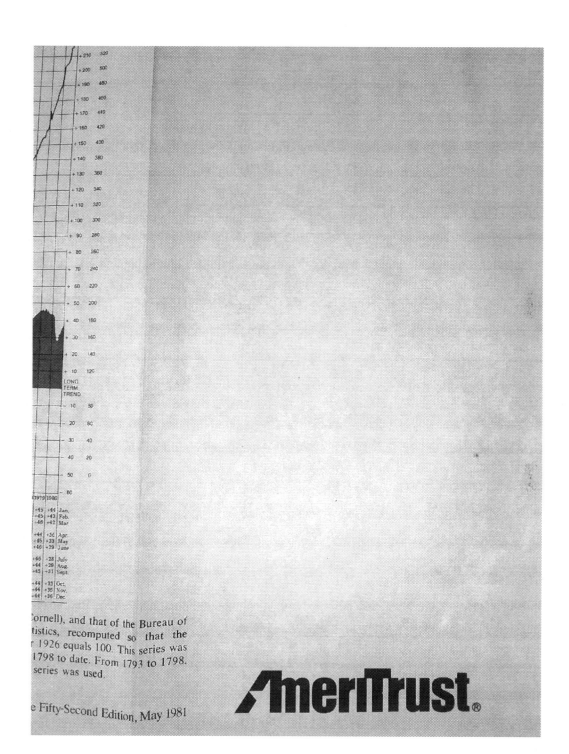

	+210	520	
	+200	500	
	+190	480	
	+180	460	
	+170	440	
	+160	420	
	+150	400	
	+140	380	
	+130	360	
	+120	340	
	+110	320	
	+100	300	
	+90	280	
	+80	260	
	+70	240	
	+60	220	
	+50	200	
	+40	180	
	+30	160	
	+20	140	
	+10	120	
LONG TERM TREND			
	10	80	
	20	60	
	30	40	
	40	20	
	50	0	
	60		

1979	1980	
+49	+44	Jan.
+45	+43	Feb.
+46	+42	Mar.
+44	+36	Apr.
+45	+33	May
+46	+29	June
+46	+28	July
+44	+29	Aug.
+45	+31	Sept.
+44	+35	Oct.
+44	+35	Nov.
+44	+36	Dec.

Cornell), and that of the Bureau of
tistics, recomputed so that the
r 1926 equals 100. This series was
1798 to date. From 1793 to 1798.
series was used.

e Fifty-Second Edition, May 1981

A clearer more substantial picture might come from the past two hundred years, compiled in a chart by Ameritrust, Figure 1.(See my book <u>High Profits In Uncertain Ttimes</u>).

The chart depicts American Business Activity from 1790 to 1980. It is full of footnotes, of interest mostly to arcane economists. The main points it makes is that there is a steady but volatile uptrend in American business. The main, horizontal line represents the long term trend in business, which they don't explicitly disclose, but I estimate at around 5% per year (2% inflation, 3% productivity increase).

The volatility about this trend is astounding.

Several war events, not including the U.S., start off the chart. England-France War, French hostilities and a peace treaty acts as negatives on the U.S. Economy. Balancing those are trading times (seaborne and trade prosperities, and maritime commerce, in the early 1800s) Later, British embargoes and the War of 1812 hamper business progress.

You can see the back and forth of good business news: a land boom, a cotton boom, another war(with Mexico), and a gold rush period. But panics also ensue, along with debt buildup. All due to the business cycle boom and bust.

Internal problems insert themselves with the U.S. Civil War in 1861, with terrible loss of life and price inflation. After the war there is a pent up expansion, geographically and business wise, plus two successive depressions (probably caused again by overly aggressive business expansion).

A long general period of upwards growth follows late into the nineteenth century producing industrial over expansion, more gold rushes, a railroad boom, corporate prosperity, mergers(oil, railroads, etc.) along with several panics: a silver campaign; rich man's panic(how is that possible?).

Another big war (World War 1) followed with attendant corporate and personal prosperity, along with wholesale price binges and a postwar depression, plus a forewarning pandemic, the Spanish Flu. They didn't have the medicine and knowledge then, but what is the excuse for the COVID 19, now?

Since World War 1, there have been big expansion periods with large depressions/recessions, all lasting more time than before. The war ended and built up substantial demand and supply, new inventions, and a long period of prosperity occurred.

Then came the big one: the Depression of 1929, caused by overbought and speculative stocks, credit over extension, and a mood of giddiness. What a whopper it was – a drop of 90% from 1929 peak to 1932 trough, making for great economic distress and wealth destruction. To this day investors greatly fear returning crunches of great magnitudes and hence many individuals and institutions are risk averse, sometimes extremely so. This is a main reason for my risk mitigating approaches, later.

World War 2, a result of depression throughout the world, obversely fueled then and thereafter an economic explosion, still felt in developed and developing countries to this day. After a brief but searing (inflation and interest rate rises) lull in the 1970s, worldwide economic growth grew steadily and many individuals and nations really prospered.

The question is, will this world-wide drumbeat continue permanently and significantly upwards?

I affirm yes, it will, mainly because of the complexity and sophistication we have reached world wide, despite business cycles and conflicts.

The Stock Market

The general analysis above is logical and heuristic, but the proof is in specific financial numbers. I now turn to the Dow Jones Industrial Averages. Started in 1896, it is a reasonable representation of (large cap) stock activity and has the longest record.

Fig. 2 (courtesy MicroTrends) depicts the Dow Jones Industrial Average from 1915-2020, on a monthly basis, in logarithmic form.

Two facts speak from this time period: one huge collapse of 90% in the late 1920s to 1932: and a steady strong upturn from 1932 to now. There were several large relapses during the upclimb: the 1970s, when turmoil and inflation prevailed; in the turn of the twenty-first century with an unsustainable growth spurt ("irrational exuberance"), in 2008-9 due to mortgage and speculative problems; and one currently due to the corona virus.

There were probably one or two devastating depressions during the 1800s, due to conflicts(civil war) and over expansions, but we're not really aware because data are sparse and incomplete.

Will there be huge drops(80-90%) in the future?

Probably not, because of the large and growing, interconnected global economy, and advanced economic and governmental tools, but I do expect some occasional large drops(40-50%) because of business cycles and conflicts.

My hypothesis is that there is a *natural growth* rate for the global economy. Anything above that rate for an extended period brings about corrective forces and the economy adjusts downwards as much as needed to bring it back on track (like a rubber band, the more the stretch, the more the snap back). We've seen that repeatedly, and for good economic reasons(competition, and supply-demand adjustments) in economics and stocks.

What is the natural rate? Probably averaging around 5% per year, reflecting population growth(2%) plus productivity(3%).

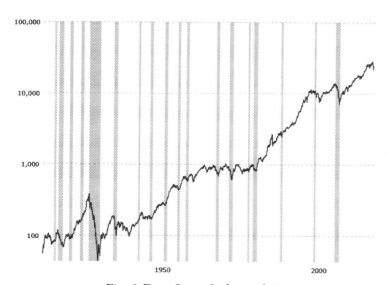

Fig. 2 Dow Jones Industrial Ave

Rises And Falls

Turn to Table 1 from my book <u>Bad Times, Great Markets</u> to discuss growths and decays in the market, as represented by the Dow Jones Industrial Average. We'll use these numbers later on to devise sell stop losses and buy stop market reentries (Chapter Three, <u>Better Methods For Returns And Risk</u>).

The table records peaks, troughs, drop sizes, and drop durations. Averages are listed at the end of the table. We can use them, with a little formula, to predict future values of those statistics with certain probabilities of occurring. For instance, we'll find out how big drops and rises can become.

The first peak we find occurs on January 2, 1929 (Remember, we start the Dow Jones Industrial series just prior to 1929, so the peak occurs, appropriately, early in 1929), at 317.51. The index drops down and hits bottom on 3/1/1929 at 308.85 (We are looking at month beginning prices, nothing in between, so all peaks occur at month's beginning).

The recovery time, from the last peak on1/02/1929 to the next peak, April 1, 1929, takes 3 months. The rise, in percentage terms, from the trough at 308.85 to the new peak of 319.29 on 4/01/1929, is 3.4%. I t only takes one month (rise time) to recover from the bottom to the new peak(319.29). Finally, and perhaps of keenest interest is the drop from peak(317.51 on 1/02/1929), of size 2.8%, which lasted 2 months(from ½/1929 to 3/1/1929).

Table 1
DJIA
Peaks/
Troughs

Date	Peak	Trough	1928-2008 Recovery Time(mos)	Rise %	Rise Time(mos)	Drop %	Drop Time(mos)
1/2/1929	317.51						
3/1/1929		308.85	3	3.4	1	2.8	2
4/1/1929	319.29						
5/1/1929		297.41	2	27.7	3	6.9	1
8/1/1929	380.33						
6/1/1932		42.84	278	861.4	269	88.7	34
2/1/1955	411.87						
3/1/1955		409.7	2	3.8	1	0.6	1
4/1/1955	425.65						
5/2/1955		424.82	2	10.2	2	0.2	1
8/1/1955	468.18						
10/3/1955		454.87	3	7.4	2	2.8	2
12/1/1955	488.4						
1/3/1956		470.74	3	9.6	3	3.6	1
4/2/1956	516.12						
5/1/1956		478.05	3	8.1	2	7.4	1
7/2/1956	517.81						
12/2/1957		435.69	26	38.5	9	15.9	17
2/2/1959	603.5						
3/2/1959		601.71	2	12.2	4	0.3	1
7/1/1959	674.88						
9/1/1959		631.68	5	7.5	3	6.4	2
12/1/1959	679.36						
9/1/1960		580.14	17	24.1	11	14.6	9
8/1/1961	719.94						
9/1/1961		701.21	3	4.3	4	2.6	1
12/1/1961	731.14						
6/1/1962		561.28	21	34.6	16	23.2	6
10/1/1963	755.23						
11/1/1963		750.23	2	8.4	4	0.7	1
3/2/1964	813.29						
4/1/1964		810.77	2	3.7	3	0.3	1
7/1/1964	841.1						
8/3/1964		838.48	2	4.4	1	0.3	1
9/1/1964	875.37						
10/1/1964		873.08	4	3.5	4	0.3	1

Table 1
<u>DJIA</u>
<u>Peaks/</u>
<u>Troughs</u>

1928-2008

Date	Peak	Trough	Recovery Time(mos)	Rise %	Rise Time(mos)	Drop %	Drop Time(mos)
1/2/1929	317.51						
3/1/1929		308.85	3	3.4	1	2.8	2
4/1/1929	319.29						
5/1/1929		297.41	2	27.7	3	6.9	1
8/1/1929	380.33						
6/1/1932		42.84	278	861.4	269	88.7	34
2/1/1955	411.87						
3/1/1955		409.7	2	3.8	1	0.6	1
4/1/1955	425.65						
5/2/1955		424.82	2	10.2	2	0.2	1
8/1/1955	468.18						
10/3/1955		454.87	3	7.4	2	2.8	2
12/1/1955	488.4						
1/3/1956		470.74	3	9.6	3	3.6	1
4/2/1956	516.12						
5/1/1956		478.05	3	8.1	2	7.4	1
7/2/1956	517.81						
12/2/1957		435.69	26	38.5	9	15.9	17
2/2/1959	603.5						
3/2/1959		601.71	2	12.2	4	0.3	1
7/1/1959	674.88						
9/1/1959		631.68	5	7.5	3	6.4	2
12/1/1959	679.36						
9/1/1960		580.14	17	24.1	11	14.6	9
8/1/1961	719.94						
9/1/1961		701.21	3	4.3	4	2.6	1
12/1/1961	731.14						
6/1/1962		561.28	21	34.6	16	23.2	6
10/1/1963	755.23						
11/1/1963		750.23	2	8.4	4	0.7	1
3/2/1964	813.29						
4/1/1964		810.77	2	3.7	3	0.3	1
7/1/1964	841.1						
8/3/1964		838.48	2	4.4	1	0.3	1
9/1/1964	875.37						
10/1/1964		873.08	4	3.5	4	0.3	1

Date						
4						
2/1/1965	903.48					
3/1/1965		889.05	2	3.7	1	1.6	1
4/1/1965	922.31					
6/1/1965		865.03	5	10.7	4	6.2	2
10/1/196 5	960.82					
11/1/196 5		946.71	2	3.9	2	1.5	1
1/3/1966	983.51					
9/1/1966		774.22	34	27.2	26	21.3	8
11/1/196 8	985.08					
6/1/1970		683.53	48	49.2	30	30.6	19
12/1/197 2	1020.02					
9/2/1974		607.82	129	101.7	103	40.4	21
4/4/1983	1226.2					
5/2/1983		1199.98	2-	2.8	2	2.1	1
9/1/1983	1233.13					
10/3/198 3		1225.2	2	4.1	2	0.6	1
11/1/198 3	1276.02					
5/1/1984		1104.85	14	16.5	8	13.4	4
1/2/1985	1286.77					
4/1/1985		1258.06	4	7.1	3	2.2	3
7/1/1985	1347.45					
9/3/1985		1328.63	3	36.9	6	1.4	2
3/3/1986	1818.61					
4/1/1986		1783.96	2	6.1	2	2	1
6/2/1986	1892.72					
7/1/1986		1775.31	2	6.9	1	6.2	1
8/1/1986	1898.34					
9/2/1986		1767.58	3	8.3	2	6.9	1
11/3/198 6	1914.23					
12/1/198 6		1895.95	2	21.6	3	1	1
3/2/1987	2304.69					
4/1/1987		2286.36	3	16.5	4	0.8	1
8/3/1987	2662.95					
11/2/198 7		1833.55	24	49.3	21	31.2	3
8/1/1989	2737.27					
1/2/1990		2590.54	9	12.1	4	5.4	5
7/2/1990	2905.2					
10/1/199 0		2442.33	8	19.3	5	16	3
3/1/1991	2913.86					
4/1/1991		2887.87	2	4.8	1	0.9	1
5/1/1991	3027.5					
6/3/1991		2906.75	2	4.7	2	4	1
8/1/1991	3043.6					
9/3/1991		3016.77	2	1.7	1	0.9	1
10/1/199	3069.1					

Date							
11/1/1991		2894.68	2	12.9	3	5.7	1
2/3/1992	3267.67						
3/1/1992		3235.47	2	5	3	0.9	1
5/1/1992	3396.85						
10/1/1992		3226.28	10	6.5	10	5	5
3/1/1993	3435.11						
4/1/1993		3427.55	2	2.9	1	0.2	1
5/3/1993	3527.43						
6/1/1993		3516.08	2	3.8	2	0.4	1
8/2/1993	3651.25						
9/1/1993		3555.12	2	11.9	4	2.6	1
1/1/1994	3978.36						
6/1/1994		3624.96	13	29.9	13	8.9	2
7/1/1995	4708.47						
8/1/1995		4710.56	2	3.9	2	2.1	1
9/1/1995	4789.08						
10/2/1995		4755.48	2	17.5	5	0.7	1
3/1/1996	5587.14						
4/1/1996		5569.08	2	1.5	2	0.3	1
5/1/1996	5654.63						
7/1/1996		5528.91	2	18	4	2.2	2
11/1/1996	6521.7						
12/2/1996		6448.27	2	6.6	2	1.1	1
2/1/1997	6877.24						
3/3/1997		6583.48	2	24.9	4	4.3	1
7/1/1997	8222.61						
10/1/1997		7442.08	7	21.8	6	9.5	3
4/1/1998	9063.37						
8/1/1998		7539.07	7	24.1	5	16.8	4
1/4/1999	9358.83						
2/1/1999		9306.58	2	15.9	2	0.6	1
4/1/1999	19789.04						
5/3/1999		10559.74	2	3.9	2	2.1	1
6/1/1999	10970.8						
9/1/1999		10336.95	3	11.2	3	5.8	3
12/1/1999	11497.12						
9/3/2002		7591.93	81	66.2	52	34	33
1/3/2007	12621.69						
2/1/2007		12268.63	3	6.5	4	2.8	1
5/1/2007	13627.64						
7/2/2007		13211.99	2	5.4	3	3	2
10/1/2007	13930.01						
Ave.s			13.5	29	11.4	7.9	3.8

The first peak-to-trough-to next peak is relatively small and short. Size and duration are very much correlated: the small sized ones, numerous in occurrence, don't last long. The next one is also small and short lasting. They are so numerous (even today) most investors and traders don't remember them.

But the third one is a whopper. The granddaddy of them all, the Great Crash begins on August 1, 1929 (prices do go higher subsequently, but not on a first of the month closing basis).

The peak registers at 380.33, not to be outdone until February 1, 1955 a period of 26 years! Prices spiral and plunge downwards until June 1, 1932. The drop actually lasts only 34 months, less than 3 years. But the size is humongous: bottoming at 42.84 on June 1, 1932, the index lost almost 90%(exactly 88.7%).

There are many attempts at rallies during those almost three years: from 164 back up to 190; then 128 to 150; another from 135 to 139; from 96 to 104; and from 76 to 81, before bottoming at 42.84 on 6/1/1932.

What's important about these rallies is that *none* of them retraced even 50% of the original drop from the peak of 380.33. Only on August 1, 1951, the Dow finally retraced more than 50%, this time on its way strongly up to make the new peak on February 1, 1951. Only once, in fact during a sizable drop (50% or more), did the average retrace 50% of its drop and fell back to new lows before recovering for good to the new peak (after the recession peak of December 1, 1972). Sounds confusing,

but we will use this weak/false recovery to tell you when when to start reinvesting in a recessionary drop(Chapter Three).

The 1929 crash bottoms on June 1, 1932, but takes 278 months from its old peak of 380.33 on June 1, 1929 to equal that old high.

The subsequent rise is mammoth, from a trough of 42.84 on June 1, 1932 to a new peak of 411.87 on February 1, 1955, a move of 861.4%. The rise, from trough to peak, lasted 260 months. So one lesson for the downtrodden, forlorn investor, is to hold his positions through the storm, and then the reward for ultimate patience is huge.

The drop, as formerly said, was 88.7%, and lasted 34 months from peak to trough. The bigger the rises, the larger the drops, but also not too long a duration. I'm not sure one can count on that statistic (short duration from peak to trough) for the future.

From that point on, the new peak of 411.87 on February 1, 1955, many peaks and troughs of small size and short duration occur. Occasionally a moderate size reaction(peak to trough) happens from time to time. In July of 1956 the Dow experienced a subsequent drop of 15.9%; another of 23.2% in December of 1961: one starting in January 1966 of 21.3%; a couple in the 1970s of 30.6% and 40.4%; another starting in August of 1987 and including the famous 1-day drop of 22% in October 1987, ultimately going down by 31.2%; a smallish one in July 1990: and finally, the tech bubble of 2000, starting in December 1999, and dropping a moderate 34% before recovering to a new peak of 12621.69 on January 3, 2007.

The averages of these statistics are recorded at the at the bottom of the table: recovery times (from peak to trough, the valley, to a new value at least equal to the old peak) averaged 13.6 months; subsequent rise sizes from trough to new peaks averaged 29 percent; rise time averaged 22.5 months; and the most important statistic, drop size, averaged 7.9%, and took 3.8 months on average to drop from peak to trough.

These figures, though interesting, have not as much importance as the projections/predictions we can make for the future. If you use the table below one can estimate with a degree of probability how big the drops will be., how long the drop will endure, recovery times, and subsequent sizes from trough to peak, both the size and duration.

For example, if we take the average drop percentage of 7.9 and multiply it by 0.7, we get 5.53%, which drop or larger should occur about 50% of the time. Likewise a drop of 1.0 times 7.9% or 7.9% or larger has a probability of occurring in the past and in the future of 37%. A drop of 3.0 times 7.9%, or 23.7%, or larger, should occur only 5% of the time. These figures can be used for the past or future.

A drop of 7.0 times 7.9%, or 55.3% or larger, has a probability of only .09% of happening. A drop 0f 10.0 times 7.9%, or 79% has only a miniscule probability of .0004 percent of occurring.

Now, obviously a big drop, 88.7% happened for the crash of 1929. That's way outside the smallest probability listed in the table above. What goes?

Two footnotes/explanations: the data in Table 1 are extensive both in number and time coverage(although in human economy time it's small, but it is all we have for anything approaching business and economic environments depicting the complex modern era). Suffice it to say an exponential distribution well describes and fits the data(hence the table above): many small-size, a moderate amount of moderate-size data, and a few big size ones. Secondly, unfortunately, as Mandelbrot(8) would say the distribution of price changes are fat-tailed, meaning more large changes occur than one would project from the mathematical distribution.

So it is for our data: big drops are bigger than called for and occur more frequently than thought. It seems there are bigger and more frequent booms and busts than we think would occur, perhaps because the economic public too easily, frequently, and strongly lusts and fears.

All these drawdowns/drops descriptions also apply to individual stocks(see my 1970 article). Go to Chapter Three for practical use of stops.

The Market Is Up!

CHAPTER TWO

Current Investment Approaches And Results

Many types of methods are used to invest in the stock markets, from academic to pundits, and everywhere in between.

Public advice and management have a checkered history.

A long time ago, in 1933, Alfred Cowles in Econometrica (see article 2) wrote that a wide range of economists to tipsters to fund managers didn't outperform the market itself, and set the stage for later studies of the same nature and conclusions, even today.

Many academics belong to the buy-and-hold school, saying the investor can't do better than just buying the market and holding on, through thick and thin. After all, you can't do better than 8% per year on average, over a long period of time. In reality, though, it is very hard for many investors to hold on through mammoth downturns like, even the long period of the 1970s, and subsequent 50% drops in 2000-2002 and 2008-9. (It is this problem/paradox that is addressed in Chapter Three).

Fama and Mandelbrot(8) were early academia to say there is much randomness in the markets and proclaim impossibility of accurate prediction, hence investment uncertainty beyond buy-and-hold strategy results. Others, like Princeton's Burton Makiel and Wharton's Jeremy Siegel concur. Yet some like Robert Schiller of Yale say investor behavior analysis show patterns and trends that analysts could pick up and perhaps profit from. On the commercial side, the late John Bogle of Vanguard Funds stated that investors can do no better than the markets and should pick market ETFs with low fees.

Then there is the Fundamental school, who believe company analysis can lead to profitable investment. Sporting a great long-term record, starting in 1965 Warren Buffet has compiled a near market matching long-term fund record using principles espoused by Graham and Dodd(6).

General funds have not done as well overall, and averaged below general market performance, much like the funds and newsletters Cowles reviwed back in 1933. Likewise with newsletters. Pundits on TV have had many recommendations but no audited records are available.

Hedge funds have also underperformed, including well known ones, averaging only 2% per year with almost that in fees, for the period 1995-2016(see Zweig(3)). A few have done spectacularly over the years, but the permanent state is debatable.(Several funds have unaudited claims, and questionable tactics that could run into trouble in years ahead: e.g. ones with frequent trading with 51% gains, 49% losses of comparable size).

Tech/Quant Methods of Investing

All of the above have different outlooks and solutions for investing: from no predictability to fancy predictive formulas for patterns and trends. The two views clash, and the verdict is still out to which is better as far as performance outcomes. Maybe it's part tradition, part technical advancement that could be forthcoming. The following gives some insight into the state of the art and science and future of technical and quantitative methods for investing. It is not anywhere exhaustive, but only representative of average practitioner's methods.

Many Timing Techniques

While there may not be as many timing methods as traders, the\re certainly are a large number, and each trader has tailored one to his liking/circumstances. Methods range from simple lines drawn on price charts to sophisticated neural nets.

Methods can be split into at least four categories: forecasting price levels; following trends; trading when no trends(randomness) are apparent; and trading special patterns/events. See Fig. 3 for a schematic of these trading methods.

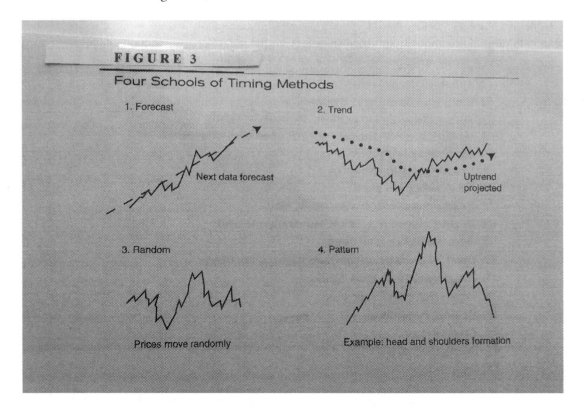

FIGURE 3

Four Schools of Timing Methods

1. Forecast — Next data forecast

2. Trend — Uptrend projected

3. Random — Prices move randomly

4. Pattern — Example: head and shoulders formation

Examples of the Forecast School

The forecasting school of stock methods has essentially two branches. One deals with data fundamental to a company's vital statistics (cash flow, industry trends, competitors, earnings, etc.).

The other technique concerns mathematical or procedural means of forecasting one or two price periods ahead, given previous price data. Of the two, the one far more often used by the trader, the mechanical approach, assumes that prices will continue to move in the latest direction by the amount forecast from the last period to the next.

The more sophisticated methods assume that prices follow a non-linear or curving growth pattern, like sine waves. All forecasts have errors, and the major problem is determining how big a risk to take when prices are out of line with the next forecast. The trader doesn't know if that error represents an opportunity(bargain price) or an ominous turn in direction(counter trend).

The purpose of the forecast is to tell the trader when prices are considerably different at the next forecast, which represents "bargain" prices, or whether prices are really turning counter to the present direction/location. He usually will buy at the bargain price, hold until the forecast has been met, and then sell. Fundamental approaches and the adaptive forecast method are two examples of this school of thought.

While used heavily in industry, quantitative forecast methods have been little employed in stocks and commodities. Two types of forecast are discussed here. Fundamental forecasting emphasizes the judgmental use of economic data; adaptive forecasting concentrates on quantitative methods.

Fundamental Forecasting

Perhaps the major difference between fundamentalists and technical methods traders is the data used and the methods of interpretation. Fundamentalists use primarily supply and demand and basic company information over longer periods(months and years), while technical practitioners utilize price data for shorter periods almost exclusively.

Methods of fundamental analysis vary, from simple rule-of-thumb or personal interpretation to more sophisticated methods like correlations and regressions. The fundamentalist tries to predict for a point much later in time using basic company factors like earnings, dividends, interest rates, cash flow, etc. and take a long position if prices are below the current forecast.

Adaptive Forecasting

An important school of prediction called exponential smoothing was pioneered in the early 1950s by R.G. Brown and was applied to industrial applications, space trajectories, and some business sales forecasting.

Essentially, exponential is a sophisticated smoothing indicator, somewhat akin to moving averages. The mathematical representation takes the form

$S = aX+(1-a)Sp$

where

a=weight(0 to 1.0) placed on the latest price (known as the smoothing factor)

X = latest price
Sp=previous smooth price
S=current smooth price
and to start things off,
S1=the first smooth price = X1, the first price

Like a moving average, the smoothed price S tends to lag behind the data, although it bends and twists and responds to data changes much more quickly. For instance, a trader doesn't have to wait for 10 data to obtain a reasonably accurate accurate 10-data smooth: only 2 or 3 prices are needed.

Many practitioners use the exponential smooth to indicate a direction of the data, not necessarily a precise forecast. This is perhaps the most significant difference that separates the utility of exponential smooths from moving averages: moving averages assume the trend of data will continue, on average, as either the unweighted average of the last N number of data, or at least the direction the direction indicated from current to last data(the beginning). Adaptive forecasts, however, learn from previous mistakes. The formula for S allows the new forecast to be influenced partly by the current data, plus a correction or addition of a part of previous forecasts(which also have learned from their past).

The major problem with this representation, however, is its inability to properly forecast ahead of the current data. In cases where prices continue going upwards, albeit sometimes even at accelerated paces, the forecast can never catch up. The same goes for plunging prices. The formula works best in moderately undulating markets going basically sideways.

One (my)modification that can allow forecasts to project ahead of current data and yet respond accurately to undulating, sideways periods is to project the next data as being equal to the current one plus a change due to the most recent pull or direction change:

$F = X + (S-Sp)$

where

F= the new data forecasting

S-Sp = the change, or difference, of current smooth less previous smooth

X= current data

As prices pull away from sideways price movements, future forecasts will adjust for the pull and calculate the next forecast as an adjusted, smooth amount added on to the current(price) data. If the data(prices) retract along the way, the next forecast will adjust for this contraction. In trading markets, the next forecast will tend to come closer and closer to prior prices as successive differences approach zero.

A trader can use these forecasts in several ways. The first is to buy when current prices are well below the next forecast by either a minimal profit amount or a small probability of prices continuing at current levels by the next period, and sell out at or near the next forecast. He can also combine forecasts with other trend methods that indicate drifts in progress, taking positions in favor of the of the trend with limited price objectives. Or he can take a position in the direction of the forecast and hold on until the forecast direction changes significantly, in effect having an open ended price objective(a buy or sell position). Finally, if he ascribes to the random walk of market price behavior, he may want to take a position opposite to the forecast direction (forecast less current price = forecast direction) if there is sufficient profit and he firmly believes near-term future prices will retreat back towards current prices.

Examples of Trend Following School

The most popular of timing techniques, trend following, as well as detecting methods, have been around for many years and have many advocates.

The Federal government uses trend following techniques frequently. Most people know of general economic trend indicators such as price index, cost of living, GDP, PPI, employment stats, and so on. But methods of analysis for these indicies are pretty crude. Several months of changes in a row typically mean(to the government official) a major change in direction.

Trend following methods range from drawing lines through the core of prices or drawing lines that touch succeeding bottom prices, to mathematical formulas(e.g. moving averages) that represent the current trend. A set of trend detecting methods uses mathematical statistics to test whether current prices are really different from the prior trending direction of prices. These methods tend to look for groups of price changes or events that tip(indicate) the direction of stock price movement.

Forecasts take no interest in the direction per se of prices, and often assume no trend or drift in prices, but rather are concerned with whether prices are outside of its channel of movement (instead looking for above and below the next the next forecast), and therefore candidates for bargain buying or selling.

Trend following and detection methods, however, predicate price buying and selling opportunities in relation to starting and stopping (and reversing) of major trends or drifts in prices. Moving averages, breakout methods, and statistical testing methods are examples of this train of thought.

The Moving Average Approach

This method is very popular amongst "technical" practitioners in the markets. It is easy to formulate in quantitative terms and is less open to interpretation than other methods. It can be easily backtested and manipulated on computers, and thus many analysts use this method to trade. Computer simulations can tell the analyst gains, losses, open account values, growth, risk, and so on a a day-to-day basis.

The assumption is that moving average line of current prices represents the current growth line of the trend. If current prices diverge significantly from this growth trend, below the average line in a bull trend or above the average line in a bear market, the current trend is then suspect, and a change in current prices to a new, opposite trend has probably occurred.

An analogy with an assembly line is a good one. If too many of the sampled products on the assembly line(too much of the price series) are defective (violate the the trend line, the conveyor belt and production process (current major trend) are halted (the trader closes out or reverses his current position).

Fig. 4 shows essentially the moving average process. In example (1) a bull trend is in effect until prices intersect the moving average at point X. A new market (downtrend) is in effect in (2) until point Y, where current prices cross over the moving average, thus indicating the probable birth of a new uptrend (bull market).

Construction/calculation of the moving average is easy. The trader first specifies the number of prices in his average. If he stipulates a large number (e.g. 100), the moving average line formed will be conservative; he believes the growth line of the trend is slowly varying and is small in growth. This means the growth doesn't change with one or two price changes, only with a large number and over a long time. Also, the rate of growth is fairly small and probably reflects a long-term, annualized growth rate.

On the other hand, if he specifies few (e.g. 5 or 10) prices in the average, he believes the growth line is volatile and depends on almost day-to-day price making events. Similarly, the growth rate is assumed high, reflecting the short-term impact of a momentous single event (e.g. a radically different earning report or a volatile international crisis).

Once he has specified the number N in the averages, the trader plots a point as the moving average for each date. The number is arrived at by dividing the sum of the closing price for that date plus the previous N-1 closing prices, by the total number of prices N.

Breakout Methods

There are probably more users of this approach than there are of all other technical methods combined.. Many prefer it because of the ease of construction and use., while many like it as the opposite of the random walk model (see next discussion).

Some use it plain: Any price move that breaks trading range highs or lows indicates a trend starting in that direction. Others prefer it fancy: Prices have to move in steps, so much up, so much down, then hold firm; and finally make a breakaway, where they must break highs or lows by so much for a new trend to be declared.

This technique is quite opposite to the no-trend method, which assumes any breakout to be a random event, where prices will ultimately return to the original state or price level. The breakout method, however postulates that a new, counter trend is just getting underway.

Figure 5 portrays two basic breakout situations. Case (1) shows essentially a breathing spell for an uptrend (bull market), a trading area in which profits are being taken by bulls and/or new shorts are entering in hopes that the last high proves to be a turning point leading to the start of a new (bear) trend. But prices stabilize, a low is formed and not violated, and prices edge up and break through to new high ground after point A.

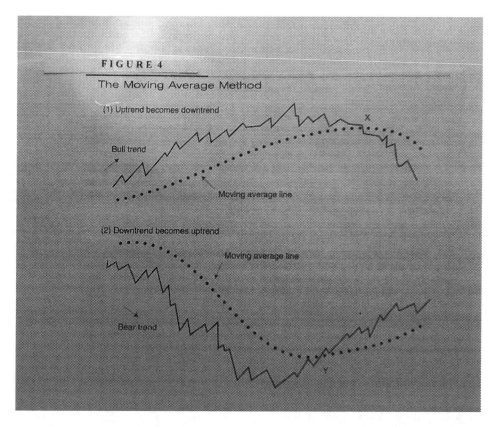

FIGURE 4

The Moving Average Method

(1) Uptrend becomes downtrend

Bull trend

X

Moving average line

(2) Downtrend becomes uptrend

Moving average line

Bear trend

Y

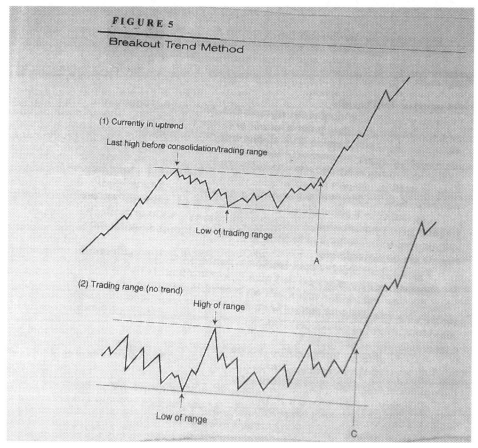

FIGURE 5

Breakout Trend Method

(1) Currently in uptrend

Last high before consolidation/trading range

Low of trading range

A

(2) Trading range (no trend)

High of range

Low of range

C

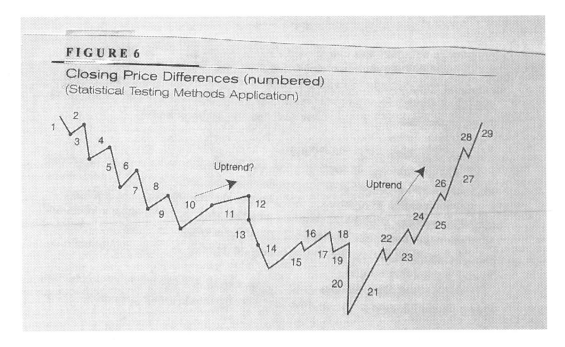

FIGURE 6

Closing Price Differences (numbered)
(Statistical Testing Methods Application)

Case (2) shows a breakout from a trading range between A and B. Prices trade between the two boundaries A and B for a long time, then break through at point C, the ceiling established before at point B.

A number of strategies lend themselves to these breakouts. The one used most frequently is to go long whenever current prices pierce the old high barrier (at A in case(1) and at B in case(2)), perhaps by a minimum amount X%. This strategy assumes prices are on their way to drifting/moving higher and, at some time in the future, establishing a new trading range.

In fact, the entire market could be looked at (especially by a random walk theorist) as a collection of trading ranges and drifts of prices pieced together. That is, one could could postulate that prices are most often in trading ranges(some say 70 percent of the time) and in disequilibrium (moving to higher/lower trading ranges or trending/drifting that way) a small amount of the time.

Another set of strategies is predicated on patterns or ways of breaking out of trading ranges. Some traders hold that breaking away from a trading range by even a certain amount is not significant in itself – the move could simply be a random move in an essentially stable price area, and the last high and low prices of the range were not good measures of the boundaries of the range of the current price equilibrium.

These traders would suggest some more sophisticated means of detecting an equilibrium price level shift. Some possible alternatives: the amount of time spent outside a trading range to assure a high probability that the newly suspected drift was real; or the *way* prices break out of trading ranges – a persistent making of new highs outside the range might suggest more significance/reliability.

An example of the way breakouts can be more reliable forecaster of trends is a mountain/ valley approach approach used for day trading that looks for a fixed number (say 5or 6) of successively new higher closings to define a new uptrend, and the same number of successively lower closings to indicate a a new downtrend. Its purpose is to filter out one-day Johnnies, those price spikes that are false indicators of trend reversals.

Statistical Testing Methods

We live in a world of uncertainty, where events are only probable at best. A team winning a championship, or even just one game; a safe journey from home to work; a city able to pay off its bonds each year; even the sun rising tomorrow are only probable events (some more than others, of course).

We should view investment price action in the same vein – uncertainty reigns. One can't draw lines on graphs or construct moving averages and expect prices to adhere to a chartered course, or "dance to our tune". All the charts and fundamental information in the world won't tell us what will happen for sure tomorrow. The best one can hope for is to estimate the *probability* of something occurring.

It is more beneficial to use methods that analyze price data and tell us the liklihood of a fall or rise.

Figure 6 displays a string of closing prices labeled 1-29 (changes were arrived at by simply subtracting yesterday's close price from that for today). This gives us a direction (sign) and magnitude of net price movement. In a way, it is an indicator of present tendency for prices: whether they are heading up or down, and for how much.

One approach to finding and timing trends would be to continually test all sorts of price differences groupings to see whether they differ significantly from the bulk of those that precede them and that constitute the present trend. In the figure, we continually test for a new uptrend, possibly one after a group (8 and 9) is formed (but probably does not pass the test).

When a significant change for a new group is found (19-27), a new trend is presumed to have started, and a trading position (here a long) is taken in the direction of the new trend. This process is repeated until a significant change in the current trend to an opposite one is determined again statistically, and then the current position is reversed.

One test that is relatively simple in terms of computation but applies broadly to varying types of data is the run-of -sign test. We essentially examine the series of price changes: when there are at least N number of successive price changes of like sign (e.g. 5 or 6 negative price changes in a row) we establish a position in the direction of the sign (e.g. go short for the above example). This is similar to getting 10 heads in a row in a coin toss or 10 reds in a row on a roulette wheel- it indicates something suspicious or non-random in the process (bad coin or wheel, or downtrend in our price change example). Other, more sophisticated statistical tests abound. For example, the G-test looks at sign and range of data all lumped into one statistic as suitable for overall data trend identification.

Examples of the No-Trend or Random School

Academics have conducted voluminous studies to show that, over the long run, price changes are not predictable from prior price changes. They stress that these changes simply discount events that randomly impinge on the marketplace each day. This effectively shoots down the trend following and forecast schools of thought, for randomists claim there are no causal trends (one set of price changes leads to another in the same direction, so it is of no use to utilize trend seeking methods in the first place.

The best one can do, they say, is to take advantage of abnormal prices outside or near a channel of prices: that is, to sell prices near the top of the channel and buy back near the bottom in anticipation that prices will return to the middle of the channel or perhaps lower.

In sum, sell strong rallies and buy sharp dips in anticipation of a reversion to more normal prices. This implies that the strength of a current rise or fall has no lasting economic meaning. The only thing a trader can count on is that prices will eventually come back to his position entrance price and perhaps better. Contrary opinion and oscillators are examples of this way of thinking.

The RSI Method

The Relative Strength Index (RSI) is an indicator generally used to seek out over bought and oversold conditions, although it could also be used in the traditional trend mode.

It measures the strength of upside movement versus the total of upside and downside price change magnitudes over an interval of time. Formally, it is the average of positive price change magnitudes divided by the average of positive and negative price change magnitudes, times 100. When it is near 100 it is considered overbought (when there are too many positive price changes in a row, prices are vulnerable to downwards moves, or negative price changes) and should be sold; while near zero (all current price changes are negative) it is thought to be temporarily oversold, and thus the stock should be bought.

Fig. 7 details this method. A downwards slanting price movement bottoms and sharply turns upwards, where (at the end when prices are streaking straight upwards) the RSI turns high positive (near 100) and thus indicates an overbought condition, so the trader goes short at the current price.

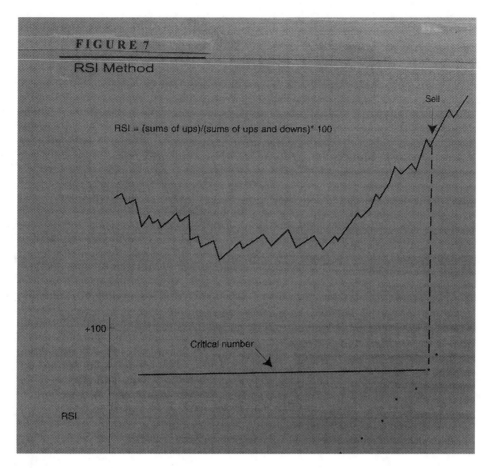

FIGURE 7

RSI Method

RSI = (sums of ups)/(sums of ups and downs)* 100

Sell

+100

Critical number

RSI

Contrary Moving Average

Ironically the moving average concept can be used both as a trend following mechanism and as a contrary, or oppositely directed, price strategy. Its best use as a trend forecasting is when trends are indeed long term and large. A long term moving average catches this situation very nicely because it filters out all noise/extraneous price movements below the average (price cycles lasting less than the length of the moving average – e.g. a 100-day average would screen out 50 day up and down trends).

But a short term average (say 5-day) would fail miserably in a sideways market that the longer term (say 100-day) average would avoid; it would get whip-sawed mercilessly after reacting to minor undulations and thus too frequently reversing positions.

This is a really perfect opening, however, to seize upon a gross negative and make it a nice, positive, profit making opportunity. One can play these temporarily overbought/oversold situations the other way: Instead of going in the direction of the immediate breakout or swing, when the moving average is relatively strong, the trader can assume the opposite price move will now occur (a move away from strength to weakness and short the temporarily strong move, thus assuming it will react soon the other way with an opposite move (here down) against the current strength.

Fig. 8 aptly describes this short-term phenomenon. Prices move very quickly in a short cycle(say, 10 days) and our valiant trader uses uses a slightly longer- term moving average (say 20 days), which would get him in a little too late on each cycle movement. At the first sell (S), prices have risen quickly and surpassed the moving average, but soon thereafter and start the down cycle. Before the average can adjust, prices have crossed on the downside, producing a loss to a previous long position. And so on through the rest of the fast cycles – the moving average is always too late – near the end of the 'faster cycle (than the moving average). But the trader should do the opposite: Instead of buying when prices break through on the upside(cross over and above the moving average), he goes *short* instead; and conversely, when prices crash through the average, he should go *long*, anticipating a quick turn of the cycle.

Examples of the Pattern School

The fourth school of thought involves belief in price patterns or events that are more complicated than mere price changes. Adherents believe certain price configurations, resembling heads and shoulders, flags, saucers and many other patterns, presage major moves and events (a major new trend or lull, for example).

Pattern recognition is a solid branch of electrical engineering applications in industry. It is used to detect the basic or underlying 'pulse' or rhythm in currents in oscilloscopes, for example. Military strategists often use it for analyzing photos from satellite reconnaisance.

In stocks, however, the state of the art is still not scientific, and great reliance is placed on the individual analyst's ability to 'see' shapes and forms in charts.

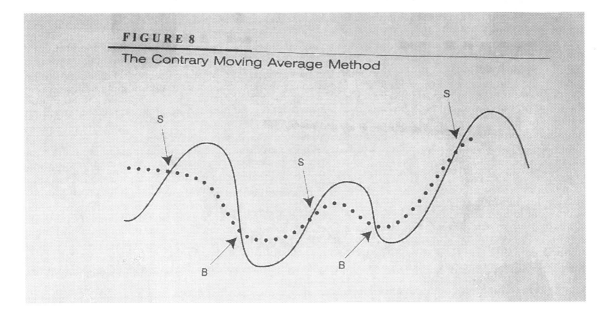

FIGURE 8

The Contrary Moving Average Method

Chart Formation

Many see the market place almost as a war between two opposing armies, one composed of bears, the other consisting of bulls. Marches are made (price wise) up and down the battlefield, with many a minor skirmish, once in a while a major battle (that is a long term trend in which bulls or bears give way to an upwards or downwards onslaught by the other side), and, finally, and end to the war.

The art of forecasting using charts depends on the recognition and interpretation of price formations that are associated historically with subsequent movement in a particular direction. Chart 1 depicts one such formation, a channel trend for cotton in 1992. The trader forms the uptrend line by drawing a line connecting subsequent reaction/drawdown lows with the top part of the channel similarly formed with intermediate high prices. The uptrend, along with prices, should grow and remain on top of the line representing the bottom of the channel of development, violation of which (by several percent, say) by subsequent prices means a new (down) trend has started.

Chart 2 shows us another telltale chart picture, a head and shoulders formation, which points the way to a trend turnaround(south) for orange juice. The left shoulder is recognized as a rally and decline of equal proportions. The head is formed by a second rally carrying beyond the first rally, but the sequent reaction carries back to where the first rally started. The right shoulder occurs when a third rally falls short of the second rally in extent, and a subsequent decline occurs that carries below the stopping points of the two previous reactions.

This formation heralds the start of an oppositely directed (down) trend, and the trader should reverse or initiate a (short) position. Some traders hold that a move equal to the second decline, from head to neckline, can be anticipated.

Wave Theories

Probably the most fascinating concept in price analysis is the theory that prices move in basic rhythms. Cycles – life and death, weather, politics, and even stock markets- are often cited.

Fig. 9 depicts three popular theories.

The Dow theory was promulgated by Charles Dow around the turn of the twentieth century and later carried on and amplified by others. Dow felt there were three waves occurring simultaneously: a major wave or trend; a minor, oppositely directed one acting against that major one; and local daily ripples or wavelets acting in all directions (see case(1)).

Most strategies connected with the Dow Theory would tell the trader in case(1) to maintain a bullish position until the minor trend became a major (bear) trend, in which case the trader should sell existing longs and go short. To recognize that change to a major (down) trend, traders would examine daily fluctuations to see whether and when they made the minor trend into a major one. Some use penetration criteria with long term moving averages, while others wait for the minor trend to grow large enough to constitute a change from minor status to major comparing minor and major trend sizes from the past. Rhea(a colleague and follower of Dow) suggests major bull trends are reversing to a bear market when succeeding bear moves in the bull trend are lower, and the same for bull moves(i.e., higher tops and bottoms of moves) in bear markets.

The Elliot wave method (2) is much more specialized and calls for exact forecasts based on the Fibonacci series of numbers, the discerning characteristic of which is that the sum of any two consecutive numbers in the series is equal to the next number: that is, 1 plus 2 equals 3, 3 plus 2 equals 5, 3 plus 5 equals 8; 5 plus 8 equals 13, 8 plus 13 equals 21, etc. (the series becomes 1,2,3 5,8,13,21, etc.).

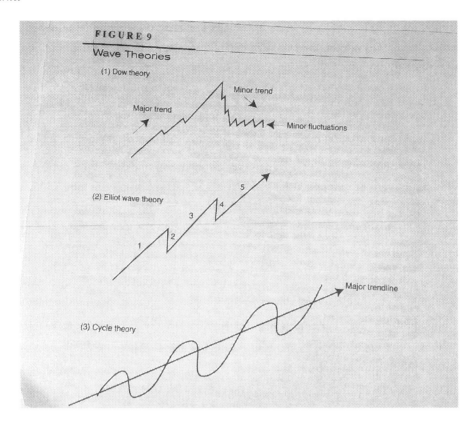

The basic rule is that the market moves upwards(1 net move) in a series of three major waves with two reaction(downwards) waves in between (see case (2) in Fig. 9). A downtrend is composed also of three moves: 2 down moves with 1 up move in between.

This theory of market behavior lends itself to forecasting strategies. If an Elliot wave is beginning, the trader can jump aboard and exit at the end of the wave(the fifth smaller wave). He may even wish to reverse position at the exit point, in anticipation of a major, reversed wave starting up.

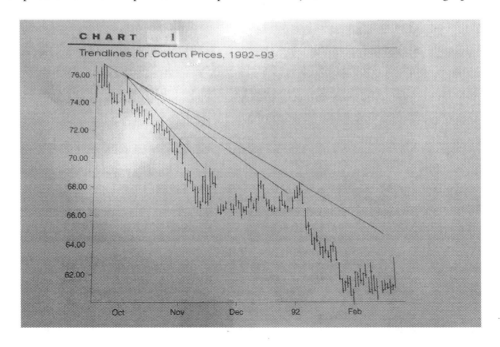

Cycle Theory

Cycle theory, represented as case (3) in Fig. 9, is a broader and more widely followed market representation than the other two wave theories

In general, cycle adherents hold that prices vacillate in drifting markets around some general trendline in a predictable, rhythmic manner. In trading ranges or non-trended markets, prices move like a sine wave on an oscilloscope, going back and forth, up and down.

The rhythmic behavior is due to the constant imbalance of buying and selling forces, which create surges one way then the other. The surges tend to alternate, even in drifting markets, because bull moves tend to cause overbought buying conditions, and bear moves bring about oversold markets – ripe conditions for buying.

Representations of cycle movements run from simply drawing tangent lines under lower and higher prices of trading ranges or trends to second-order partial differential equations which are used as sophisticated mathematical models of cycle price behavior. In one mode, or representation, the frequency of ups and downs and amplitudes (magnitudes) of the ups and downs constitute the major variables to be estimated. Sine wave, theory has wide applications in electrical engineering (for example, household current), and some have applied it to in the form of fast Fourier transforms to the markets.

Three trading strategies are generally employed with cycle theory. Traders should buy when prices come close to the low end of the channel, near the next predicted bottom, and sell when prices come close to the next projected top. In a way, this strategy is based on quality control: most prices tend to occur near the trendline, with fewer and fewer occurring farther and farther away from the trendline. The trader should expect a smaller price occurrence near the boundaries and so should take an opposite stance (sell at a higher boundary, and buy at the lower one) in anticipation of prices returning closer to the middle of the channel, or even toward the other boundary. Stops to close out the position are placed just outside the boundary.

A second trading method hypothesizes that if prices break out of the undulating channel's boundaries, then they are headed higher (upside breakout) or lower (downside breakout). This is based on the belief that the cycle model represents the current price range or trend and that any violation of the channel enveloping the range or trend means a new status for prices – a new trend, or drift. The trader takes a position in this new direction when the channel has been violated and holds the new position until a violation of the new trend envelope occurs in the opposite direction.

The third strategy involves the use of predictions. Some analysts use sinusoidal (wave) functions, others use lines to forecast the next set of tops and bottoms. The strategy used here is to buy if current prices are well below the next predicted top and sell if prices are considerably above the next predicted bottom price. The trader is essentially going for short term profits, not waiting for the long-term profits that result from a sizable drift in prices.

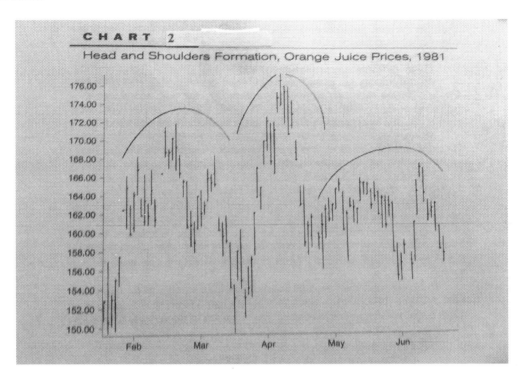

CHART 2

Head and Shoulders Formation, Orange Juice Prices, 1981

Investment Management

Whether an investor uses managers or his/her own methods, he/she has to be aware of risk and return metrics, to measure how good is the portfolio performance.

As we have seen from the first discussion, many/the majority of pundits, analysts funds, managers, and brokers have come up short, not matching the performance of the market itself. I claim that quantitative methods also come up short, partly because of inherent problems (e.g. the moving average method with numerous whipsaw losses leading to long, sustained portfolio drawdowns), and a lack of discipline using them.

Many of these shortcomings can be attributable to the client himself. Delusionary profit goals and vulnerability to risk control make him his worst enemy. "Know thyself" says the oracle. If you can truly understand what makes you tick, establishing reasonable profit goals and reasonable risk for your profile, then there are sound, reasonable plans out there. I urge you to read and adapt one or more of the strategies in Chapter Three.

Getting back to return and risk metrics, there are the usual, basic ones: total profitability, per year profit percentages, profits to losses ratios, individual gains and losses, max gain, max loss, drawdown statistics, costs(commissions and fees). Of these, total profitability, yearly return and risk statistics count most to most investors.

I would add or emphasize the risk statistics, especially the sequence or *order* of gains-losses, and the drawdown statistic.

Order of gains and losses matters a lot. The Sharpe ratio, the average return divided by the standard deviation of the returns, is simply not enough for a measure of return per risked dollar. The *order* or sequence of gains and losses is often crucial: take Portfolio A, which has returns of +6%, +6%, +6%, +6%, +6%,+6%,-3%,-3%,-3%,-3%,-3%,-3% for 12 months. Compare this to Portfolio

B, which has a sequence of returns +6%,-3%,+6%,-3%,+6%,-3%,+6%,-3%,+6%,-3%,+6%,-3% for the same 12 months.

Both portfolios have the same Sharpe ratio. Which one would you prefer? The choice isn't even close: Portfolio B!

That's because the average (and maximum) drawdown in Portfolio B is only -3%, compared to -20% for Portfolio A.

Drawdown is very important: next to total returns, the investor/manager looks to it as the most important statistic.

Also, the average drawdown is more important than the maximum drawdown, due to reliance on one data point with the maximum drawdown, but with many more numerous and as a group reliable numbers compiled in the average statistic. (See my article (1) on individual stock reactions and drawdown, and more about portfolio drawdowns in Taming The Pits)

CHAPTER THREE

Better Methods for Returns and Risk

Now that the forever nature (as long as mankind is around) of the upwards drift of the stock market is affirmed, we have to propose long position strategies with good returns and acceptable risks for each investor profile.

Here are proposed two stop strategies to help the long term investor (individual or institution) sharply *reduce risk* yet retain/improve gains, and the short term trader gain more in his portfolio while keeping risk low.

The stop strategy has had a long but inconclusive history. Many advisors, in print, on TV, and managing funds, have counseled using stops to protect against losses. No real quantitative basis has been offered. Chapter Two reviewed drawdowns from recent price peaks to bottoms for investors to expect certain price drop/retreats sizes, and probabilities. These stats can be used to devise sell stops, to protect capital against losses. On the other hand, I am *adding* here a similar construction to aid the investor *when* and *where* to initiate or return to long positions.

The buy and sell stops will combine to give the investor protection against large market price drops, even black – swan events(not expected/ predicted monster price drops, like in 1929), and preserve, even enlarge, profit results. Long only positions are initiated, as <u>Chapter One</u> and <u>Two</u> show the futility of short sales.

The following are three strategies that meet the requirements: buy–and- hold, and two stop strategies for entering and closing out stock and indicies investments.

The buy-and-hold is the simplest and many say the best to obtain superior long-term profit results. See Table 3 for buy-and-hold results for the period 1915-2020.

The Adjusted Nominal Fraction (ANF) is the fractional return on $1 starting point to the end of the trade or period. Subtract 1 from the fraction and multiply by 100 to get the percentage return.

The Maximum Drawdown is the largest drop percentage found in the period of testing.

Essentially you buy with funds you then have available to buy a Dow Jones Industrial Average ETF (like the DIA), or S&P 500 ETF (SPY) or other like general market indicie, and hold the position until you die (pass on to heirs, essentially) or cash in on a real emergency.

The account would have gained 41,899% by buying at 56.5 on 1915-01-01 close, and selling at 23,723.69 on 2020-6-01. Very good! Depending on starting dates, you would have earned an average of about 8% per year!

On the negative side, you would have had to endure a devastating drop of 90% in the account by 1932, and nearly 23 years before returning (1951) to prior (1929) highs. Also, from about 1965 to 1982, 17 years, you would have seen drops of 50% value several times to your account. Likewise, from 2000-2004 a similar fate would have occurred: a 50% drop in value and four more years of waiting. Another drop of 50% would finally occur in 2008-9, and relief for ten years until now, in 2020, when a (still occurring drop of 25% happened due to the corona virus (COVID 19).

The buy and hold investor would have to have steel nerves and extreme faith in this long-term method. And lots of patience.

Not many can faithfully adhere to this approach.

That is why I am exploring some *improvements* to the buy-and-hold method, to *reduce* portfolio losses significantly and possibly *improve* upon profit performances.

I found efficiencies in price drops and recoveries, in that good stops could reduce losses before bottoms were hit, and improve long position reentry on the upside recovery, using stops.

The whole concept revolves around using stops to reduce losses and improve gains. Buy stops to enter positions, sell stops to exit them.

There are two stops, in this 1915-2020 data, used on a monthly (1st of the month closing basis): a sell stop initially placed X% below the price the DJIA was bought, and moved up and placed X% below; the first and succeeding *higher* monthly(first of the month) closing bases; and a buy stop figured from from new, lowest bottoms (see Fig.10). Sounds confusing: let me further explain!

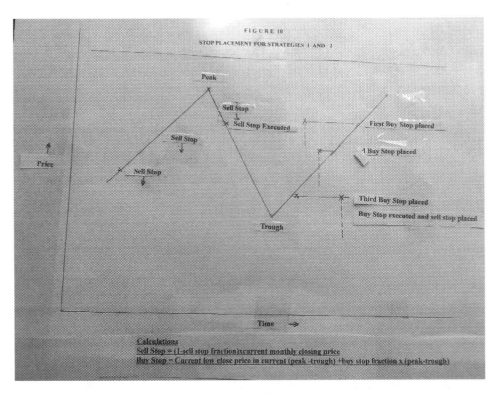

When you first enter the market (buy the Dow ETF (DIA) at the market) you should place a sell stop mentally, executable at month's end (see Chapter Five for exact instructions), X% below the entry price.

You then increase the sell stop(in your mind) as the DIA price rises at each month's close, to newer highs (no matter how much higher), placing the sell stop X % below the new high close. (See successively higher sell stop placements at points 1, 2 and 3 in Fig. 10)

Finally, when the current DIA monthly closing pieces falls below the last sell stop, you quickly sell your long position at the market, at that close or as soon as possible. Because of the nature of DIA trading(very liquid), you should get close to the month's closing price. If not, you should get that price as an average over time (e. minus 2%, plus 3%, minus 1 %, plus 1%, etc., averaging to close to zero percent off the actual monthly closing price).

For reentry to the long position, place a buy stop(for the first stop) above your exit price, and above each succeeding *lower* monthly DIA closing price(see Fig. 10 for 3 successive buy stop placements), using a little formula I will detail in <u>Chapter Five</u>.

Eventually the DIA will reach a bottom, rise and then execute your (mental) buy stop, which you should execute, again at the market as soon as the monthly closing price exceeds your latest buy stop.

The buy stop is equal to the current lowest DIA close price after your sell stop is executed, plus the buy stop fraction times the difference between last top and current bottom of the DIA drop.

For example of a sell stop, suppose you set it at 10% of the last last monthly close price, and enter you enter the DIA at 300 (its price is only 1% of the real Dow Industrial Average of 30,000), then the first stop is 270 on the next monthly close. Subsequently the DIA monthly close rises up to 310, thus your stop is raised to 279, 10% below the new high closing of 310. A second raise in stop price occurs when the next DIA occurs at 315, so your stop is raised to 10% off then new high closing of 315, to 283.5

Finally, the DIA falls to 283 on a subsequent monthly close, and you place a market sell order and obtain, say, a position closing price of 282.5, for a loss of 5.8 % plus commissions(in today's environment, they are zero for online orders!)

For a reentry long position, we put a buy stop (mentally) initially X% (let's say 30% in our example) initially at the just closed out price plus 30% of the difference between the last top and the (first) suspected bottom(in our example the top is 315, bottom 282.5, so the buy stop= 282.5 +.30 x(315-282.5)=292.25.monthly closing price for the DIA.

If the DIA monthly closing prices subsequently drop even lower to 250, say, then lower the buy stop to (new bottom is 250, top still 315 so the buy stop now is 250+ .3x(315-250)= 269.5 on the next DIA monthly closing price.

Suppose the DIA monthly close price drops even further to 230, then the buy stop is lowered to 230+ .3x(315-230)=255.5, with the new bottom=230, top still at 315.

Finally, the DIA prices rise, and pierce through latest (mental) monthly buy stop, say to 256, in this example. A buy market order is placed immediately to reenter the long position in the DIA. Say the DIA monthly closes at 256, then the market buy order might be filled at 255, helping him to offset other poorer fills.

For stop strategies 2 and 3 (strategy 1 is the buy-and-hold one) the investor has to choose values for two variables: *sell stop* fraction size and *buy stop* fraction size. One (sell stop fraction) stipulates the loss constraint or gain preservation (give back portion of accrued gains, which can be large). The other (buy stop) stipulates the long position entry/reentry fraction, which judges how much (fraction) of the drop from peak to trough signals a return of the bull market. (See Fig. 10 where the bull stop is executed, at point z)

Some Results

The following test results are a few possibilities and neither imply that a fuller test would validate my conclusions, or are the optimum. But they do suggest plausibility and reasonability of effective stop use on the DIA, and later on for individual stocks and ETFs. They assume no commissions (a present day reality) and no average slippage (again, no verdict on that). Also, the tests are of a hindsight quality, testing the past, not vigorous testing of *future* data(see my book <u>Trading Systems Analysis </u>for price models and creation of data for testing). Testing past data, whether in samples for optimization purposes, or out of sample (different past data) forward testing is strictly verbotten for future results claims!

First, I'll note some observations about DIA past price behavior that will influence my choices for both sell and buy stops tests.

Refer back to Fig. 2 the MicroTrend DJIA price chart from 1915-2020, and Table 4 (see Appendix, MicroTrends opening day monthly closing prices digital data).

The first thing that hits us is the huge drop in 1929 and subsequent big drops in 1965, 2000, and 2009, all of long periods of time. We would like to avoid long droughts with step asides, putting money in interest bearing accounts, until viable long term uptrends begin anew. Hopefully the losses during those downdrafts can be minimized, and profits kept or possibly expanded in reentries and return to the bull market.

Analysis indicates stop losses should be limited to around 25%, lest 50% or other larger stops evaporate and render useless position step asides. We can try smaller stops, but must realize it will result in smaller losses, but more frequent trades, especially losses. I estimate stop loss percentages should range between 10% to perhaps 30-40 percent, at most. Again further testing will find optimum settings.

As for buy stops for reentry, I noticed good values between 33% and 67% for percentage of drop from recent top to bottom, that escape premature rises (say 20%) that don't truly signal a return to the uptrend (more drops to come before a real bottom occurs). See results ahead for too tight buy stops, resulting in unacceptable numbers of new losses that add up to too large a drawdown of losses!

A number of sell and buy stop combinations were tested: sell stops of 10% and 25%, which is the approximate ideal range; buy stop percentages of 33%, 50% and 67%(2/3 retracement of the drop).

I was a bit shocked and surprised to find generally good results using sell and buy stops. I had not expected anything worthwhile to help/exceed buy and hold for stocks. In my experience for commodities stops had helped with avoiding complete disasters, but I didn't think stops would help strengthen the buy-and-hold philosophy for stocks.

Was I surprised!

Stop Strategy DJIA Results

The tables that follow detail selected trading outcomes for the DJIA from 1915 to 2020. The table heading tells the sell (exit the long position) and buy (enter/reenter the long position) stop sizes chosen.

Dates and prices for entry and exits are shown, along with the trade's profit/loss. Added to the P/L is an interest rate earned on idle funds, from exit of the trade to entry of the next trade. I assume 3%

average yearly interest over the whole period, even though interest rates actually varied, with extremes of double-digit rates during the 1970s, and virtually zero interest currently

The Adjusted Nominal Fraction (ANF), the sum of P/L trade fraction and interest fraction earned on idle funds applied to the last ANF constitutes the next Adjusted Nominal Fraction. Starting at 1.0, at the end of trading, minus 1.0, times 100, shows the total percent gained. It can be compared to other strategies' results. The buy-and-hold sowed an ANF of 419.89, or 41,889% profit from 1915-2020, in Table 3.

Turning to Table 5, Trading Results for Strategy#2, 25% sell stop, 33% buy stop, we find the first trade closes out on1917-10-01 when the initial long position, established on 1915-01-01 at 56.5 is stopped out when the sell stop is raised from an initial price of 40.4 to 79.48, and executed on 1917-10-01 at 74.5 for a 32% profit. The next Adjusted Nominal Fraction is calculated to be 1.37, after earning nearly 5% in the time before the next trade begins.

The next trade is entered at 84.68 on 1919-04-01 after rising 33% of the range, from the last peak (105.97) to last trough(72.65) plus the trough price of 72.65, and stopped out at 86.85, with a P/L of 2%, and subsequent interest earned of almost 5%. The Adjusted Nominal Fraction is further increased to 1.44. And so on.

The end results are pretty encouraging: good trade success rate(61%), better than most trend following methods; large profit per trade(102%); only 2 drawdowns of 5% and 38%; and importantly a final Adjusted Nominal Fraction of 470.83, or nearly 47,000% profit from beginning to end, better than the buy-and-hod strategy (419.89).

Finally, most important, a maximum drawdown of 38%, far better than the buy-and-hold strategy (90% worst drawdown, with many drawdowns of 50% or more. But to employ this strategy, you must "work" at it, by continuously recalculating buy and sell stops(only one for each month, though), and adhering to strictly implementing the methodology. And executing executing 13 trades over 100 years(not to frequently- one every 8 years!).

Definitely a candidate system to trade, instead of the buy-and hold strategy

Table 6 presents the results for a little different stop strategy, 25% sell stop(same as Table 5), but 50% (reentry) buy stop. Table 7 shows the same (as Table 5), but with 67% (two thirds) retracement buy stop foe reentering long positions.

The results for both buy stop fractions in Tables 6 and 7 are good, but not as good as those in Table 5.

A 50% reenter fraction strategy in Table 6 produces 7 of 10 trades as profitable, or 70%, and a worst drawdown of 17%, both good numbers. But the Adjusted Nominal Fraction of 230.73 is less than that of the buy-and-hold method (419.89).

Table 7, with a 67% reentry criteria, fares even worse, with a 208.14 ANF, a worse max drawdown of 24% and three drawdowns averaging 11%. It seems the higher the reentry fraction, the worse the results.

Tables 8,9 and 10 present results for a far different sell stop loss(10%) but with the same three buy stop fractions of 33%, 50%, and 67%.

Table 8 represents the smallest stop combinations of all tables looking at trading the DJIA from a long term, uptrend perspective only. The sell stop is small, 10%, and so is the recovery/restart long position buy stop, at 33% fraction of recent top to bottom difference. This means an early stop out should a price downturn begin, and a relatively short downturn rebound to uptrend reentry requirement.

The results are spectacular! The end profit results (586.84 ANF or 58,584 % profit over the whole stretch of time) are significantly better than that for the buy-and -hold (419.89 ANF or 41,889% profit from start to finish).

Even better, the worst and average drawdowns (36% and 13%) are far better than that for the buy-and-hold (90% and around 20% for maximum and average drawdowns), including several 50% drawdowns for the B & H method.

In addition, the average profitable percentage for this approach is 55%, a good number relative to other methods, and a profit per trade of 59% It requires, though, 47 trades over more than a century, or 1 trade every 2 years, for investors to handle.

For reasons of the above statistics, I would hold this high, number one, in methods to use.

The other two settings, 10% sell stop and two possible buy stop reentry percentages of 50% and 67% of the downturn size for reentry, are depicted in Tables 9 and 10.

The results are not as good as with a *smaller* reentry buy stop of Table 5: the Adjusted Nominal Fraction (ANF) for both were worse (206.91) Table 9 and 169.46 for Table 10. But worse and average drawdowns were better, 32% and 9% for Table 9, and 22% and 9% for Table 10.

These two settings may appeal to investors who desire less trades and time preparation for each trade, and perhaps less drawdowns.

The above results for different sell and buy stop settings beg the question: how about *smaller* settings?

Right from the outset they would involve more trades, certainly, and more calculating and setting more frequently both stops (still mentally, not actual orders placed).

I did investigate some smaller settings, especially for buy stops. I did not check out lower sell stops say 5%, because I anticipated far too many and premature position stop outs, resulting in too many individual and cumulative losses. These conditions are clearly foretold by the following results with lesser buy stop settings.

Table 11 depicts the results for the 10% sell stop and 10% buy stop fractions (a very tight, quick reentry requirement). I have reversed the order of selling and buying reporting, but the results of the transactions can be easily seen, as I shall point out.

The trading is ok until mid 1930, when a losing streak starts, initially with a 15% loss on 1930-06-01, followed by -12& on 1930-09-01, -20% on 1931-04-01, -36% on 1931-09-01, and-15% on 1932-10-01 1932-10-01 also on the downside of the 1929 crash. Too many losses adding up to virtual decimation and elimination of the investor's capital. Conclusion: too many trades, making for whipsaw, cumulative portfolio losses, due to tight stops and tight reentry requirements.

Similar results occur for even a slightly higher reentry fraction (Table 12), but with fewer trades and bigger losses, culminating in four consecutive losses of -20% or more, dooming the portfolio to extinction.

Individual Stocks

What about individual stocks themselves?

Can a sell stop, buy stop strategy do well (profit and risk wise)?

We'll inquire about a period from 2000-2020, 20 years.

Tables 15-17 detail the results buy-and-hold and two stop strategies on the DIA ETF, first.

The Dow Jones Industrial, ETF (symbol DIA) starts at 10,566 on 2000-06-01 and ends at 23,723.62, a gain of 124%, or Adjusted Nominal Fraction of 2.24, starting from 1.0 (Table 15). The worst drawdown on the buy-and-hold position occurs in 2008-9, with about a 50% drop before recovering.

Table 16 shows the same period with 10% sell stop and 33% buy stop reentry fractions for the long position DIA.

The total profit performance of 100% or 2.00 ANF is roughly comparable to that for the buy-and-hold strategy, but the worst(and only) drawdown of 38% is superior to 50% for the buy-and-hold method.

Table 17 shows again about the same Adjusted Nominal Fraction returns, but with with markedly better worst drawdown of 28% instead of 50%, for the sell stop setting of 25% and 33% buy stop fraction.

Individual stocks were not extensively tested (go to Chapter Four for extensive testing on all sectors of the S&P 500) only a representative few, to get an idea of whether the concept works in theory and practice.

For the sample set of stocks, I chose a tech, financial and food products companies, for a quick general over all feel to test for profitability and risk control. Specifically, Apple (AAPL), Aflac (AFL) and Proctor and Gamble (PG).

I tried the two successful strategies of 10% sell stop, 33% buy stop reentry, and the 25% sell stop and 33% buy stop reentry strategies.

The buy and hold alone for PG produced a nice 313% profit over the 20 year time frame, for a 4.13 Adjusted Nominal Fraction. The worst drawdown was -36%, in 2005-9, on paper.

Table 18 displays trade results made with the 10% sell stop, 33% retracement buy stop. The total profit was 270% a little less than that for the buy-and-hold, but it showed less drawdown(16%) than for the B&H methodology(36%).

A better result turns up for the 10% sell stop, 33% buy stop rentry approach (Table 19); virtually comparable total profit (293%), but much lower worst drawdown: 0% on closed trades.

Table 20 and 21 show the same results for Aflac(AFL).

The buy-and-hold strategy for AFL shows an end profit of 176% for the period of 20 years, with many significant drops of 40% or more, and a maximum drawdown of 76%. Not good.

The 25% stop, 33% reentry fraction method shows in Table 20 a return of 130% for the period, but far better max drawdown statistic of no drop. And a winning trade percentage of 75%.

The tighter sell stop of 10% sell stop, 33% buy stop reentry fraction (Table 21) produces even better results: a total profit of 256%, compared to 176% for the buy-and-hold; and a maximum drawdown of 12% contrasted to 76% for the buy-and-hold philosophy.

Finally, the most interesting stock of most recent history, Apple (AAPL). . It is known for rock solid growth, volcanic price rises, bur some spectacular drops in value.

Tables 22 and 23 display the results for the two buy-sell stop strategies.

If bought outright on 2000-07-01, at 7.55, an investor would have realized 4,750% profit, or 48.9 Adjusted Nominal Fraction, by selling at the end for 369. A huge profit! But not without persistently, patiently holding on during mini-crashes of 76% in 2000, 60% in 2005, 50% drop in 2008, 50% drop in 2013, and a similar drop in 2019. A lot of faith and insight required!

Could the investor have done as well with the stop strategies?

No, not in total profitability: there is no way a methodical approach can do as well(maybe almost?) as a prescient or lucky holder of a rocket stock!

Table 22 presents results of the 10% sell stop, 33% buy stop reentry method. Total profitability in only about half (2,070%) of the buy-and-hold approach, but its worst drawdown (2000) is only 49%, and subsequent ones are few(4) and small-size (ranging from 7% to 25%. There definitely is a serious tradeoff between return and risk here!

Table 23 shows the results for a 25%sell stop, 33% buy stop reentry strategy. There is even a wider discrepancy this method and the buy-and-hold for Apple: the total return is 1,709%, still good, but less than the buy-and-hold(4,780%) and the 10% sell stop, 33% in Table 22 (2,070%). Its worst drawdown is the same as with the 10% sell stop one in Table 22, or 49%. If we had started the time frame earlier we might have experienced far less drawdowns, by virtue of only 10% and 25% trailing stops, for the respective methods.

In summary, the two stop strategies hold up well on individual stocks. For all three methods tested, they come up magnificently superior to the buy-and hold itself for these three stocks in reducing *risk*, often sizably.

As far as profitability, its a mixed bag. They show better overall returns for one(AFL), about the same for another(PG) and worse for the third (AAPL).

As shown for the DIA,(and I presume for other indicies-see <u>Chapter Four</u>), the stop strategies are superior in returns and risk performances.

It still is up to the investor or institution to decide which ones (stocks or indicies) to select for investment, and which strategy(ies) to employ, based on the return and risk profile of the investor.

For more testing results on indicies and individual stocks in different sectors, see <u>Chapter Four</u>.

More on the decisions and *how* to implement them, in <u>Chapter Five</u>.

CHAPTER FOUR

Strategy Tests On Stocks And Indicies

Now we come to some more extensive and insightful analyses. Check out Table 24 Investment Results for Three Strategies. (2000-2020). It lists results for 5-10 individual stocks in each of the nine S&P 500 sectors (IT and telecommunications were combined because I found only one telecom in the 2012 Standard and Poor's 500 Guide).

The table shows indicie or sector name, symbol, strategy used ((1) buy-and-hold; (2) 25% sell stop, 33% buy stop reentry; (3) 10% sell stop, 33% buy stop strategy), number of successful trades;; number of total trades, the maximum percent drawdown; the Adjusted Nominal Fraction(ANF) for each stock/indicie and strategy; and the maximum drawdown, in %, for that stock/indicies and strategy.

The most important/ statistics in this table are the maximum drawdown number (a risk measure) and the ANF number (a return measure).

The maximum drawdown tells us the worst percent drawdown or drop in the portfolio's value history. For example, Chevron(CVX) experienced a maximum drawdown ending on 2014/09 month closing of -40% for the buy-and-hold policy.

For the 25% sell stop 33% buy stop reentry method for CVX, the worst drawdown was -10%, starting on 2016/04 month's end, and ending on 2020/02 after the trade was stopped out at 93.81. This strategy far better than the buy-and-hold, which suffered a maximum drawdown of -40%, a huge, significant difference in the risk column (a 75% reduction in maximum loss for the period).

The ANF measure tells us the return on the stock/indicie portfolio from the beginning of the period to the end of the testing period. That is, $1 starting value ends up at $3 means the account value has trippled, or improved by 200% ($2 profit divided by 1$ invested yields 200% return on capital). In the other end of returns, an ending value of less than 1 means the portfolio lost money: e.g. a value of.7 disappoints the trader by telling him he lost (.7-1.0)x100= -30%! Yes, some stocks did lose during this time period of 20 years! (Check out GE and X)!

For Chevron, the buy-and-hold produced an ANF of 2.12, or $1.12 from the start, a gain of 112%. The ANF of the 25% sell stop 33% buy stop method yielded an ANF of 2.25, a gain of 125%, a little better than the buy-and-hold strategy.

These two statistics, maximum drawdown and ANF, represent the bottom lines of risk and return that the investor must view as most crucial to his investment performance. Of course, there are ancillary statistics to consider (such as fundamental factors like cash flow, management capability, and industry/product potential). See <u>Chapter Six</u> for a discussion of these and stock selection problems and solutions.

Analysis of Table 24

First, let's look at the indicies ETFs SPY, DIA, $COMPX(the S&P 500, Dow Jones Industrials, and the NASDAQ Composite).

The buy-and-hold plan shows 2.03 ANF or 103% return and worst drawdown of -52% for the period 2000-2020(ending June 2020 monthly closing). Strategy 25% sell stop plan by contrast shows 2.62 ANF or 162% profit and only -25% drawdown, a markedly better return and risk profile than the buy-and-hold

The 10% sell stop model does even better: 5.18 ANF or 418% return and only -4% worst drawdown, a huge improvement over the buy-and-hold plan.

For the Dow Industrial ETF (DIA), the results are mixed. All three strategies show about the same return, around 100%, but a decided improvement in maximum drawdown by the 25% and 10% sell stop strategies(-6% and -38% for the 25%sell stop and 10% sell stop programs, respectively, versus -50% for the buy-and-hold).

But the NASDAQ Composite results tell a clearly superior story for the two sell stop strategies compared to the buy-and-hold plan: only a 2.4 ANF(140% return) and -72% max drawdown for the buy-and-hold, versus 3.75 ANF(275% return) and -26 % max drawdown for the 25% sell stop model; and a 3.61 ANF (261% return) and only -1% max drawdown for the 10% sell stop one.

Turning to individual stocks *by sector,* the results are as follows: over all sectors, the sell stop strategies fare better than the buy-and -hold policy on returns (ANF) and *significantly* so on maximum drawdown, by more than 50% (-62 % for the buy-and-hold, -27% and -25% for the two 25% and 10% sell stop strategies).

By sector:

<u>Energy</u>

For the energy sector, returns average significantly better for the stop strategies than for the buy-and -hold: 163% for the 25% sell stop strategy, and a substantial 352% return for the 10% sell stop one, versus only a 99% ave increase for the B&H model.

Similarly, the stop strategies (25% and 10% sell stop, 33 % buy stop) experienced only -28% max drawdowns, versus a staggering -72% figure for the B&H.

Some individual stock results observations:

Two stocks (Chevron and Continental Phillips) showed similar ANF returns(about 100% profit returns), with 10% sell stop model lower at 36%, but much worse risk numbers of -40% and -64% max drawdown stats for the B&H, versus -10% and -25% for CVX and COP, respectively, for the 25% sell stop version, and -30% and -35% for the 10% sell stop one.

Stronger differences show up for the rest of the energy stocks(EOG, HAL, OXY, and WMB): ANF profit returns of 5.26, 5.9, and 8.6 for the B&H, 25% sell stop, and 10% sell stop methods for EOG, for instance, and max drawdowns of -73%, -24%, and -25% respectively, for the three strategies (for EOG).

Even stronger comparisons turn up for HAL(Haliburton): a loss of -50% for the B&H:; a gain of 35% for the 25% sell stop strategy; and a whopping gain of 348% for the 10% sell method. The max drawdown results are even more sharply contrasting: -91 % for the B&H, while only -34% max drawdown for both the 25% and 10% sell stop strategies.

Occidental Petroleum(OXY) also shows similar results to HAL: 71% return profit return for the B&H, 252% for the 25% sell stop approach; and a magnificent 662% return for the 10% sell stop strategy.

Even wider results occur for Williams Company (WMB) with a loss of -46% for the B&H policy, and a +7% return for the 25% sell stop, and +216% return for the 10% sell stop one. Max portfolio losses are also dramatically different, -95 % max loss for B&H, and -44% for the 25% sell stop and only -19% for the 10% sell stop model.

Financials

Overall results show a great improvement in max drawdown using the sell stop buy stop strategies, versus the buy-and-hold; to the tune of -70% (B&H), -42% (25% sell stop), and -28% (10% sell stop method).

And the returns are similarly better for the two stop methods: an ANF of 1.55 for the B&H; 1.48 for the 25% sell stop:; and 2.59 for the 10% sell stop strategy.

For individual financial stocks, the trend of better performance of reduced maximum drawdowns by the stop strategies over the B&H continued.

Bank of America (BAC) typifies this trend.

The maximum drawdown on portfolio values comes in at -93%, a perfectly horrible number, while showing considerably less with the 25% and 10% sell stop strategies, at -68% and -40%, respectively.

The ANF figures show a dramatic difference also.

BAC *loses* 10% in the time period of 20 years, while the 25% and 10% sell stop strategies show a 10% and 123% *gains*.

Similar results are found for CINF, GS, MET, and PNC for the drawdown statistics.

Mixed but generally better ANF returns show up for these stocks using the two stop strategies.

Health

Steadily better results for ANF and sharply improved max drawdown stats show up for the health industry using the stop strategies. The industry shows all around good returns, no matter which investment approach is used: returns range from 591% to 762%.. The two stop methods improve significantly for all five stocks on maximum drawdown, however: -23 % and -25% for the 25% sell stop, and 10% sell stop methods, respectively, versus -53% for the B&H method.

There are differences amongst individual stocks, however. The established, always profitable corporations like Abbot Labs and Johnson & Johnson fare very well in AFN numbers by buying and holding, compared to that for the two sell stop strategies.

A note on one stock's performance: United Healthcare (UNH) does extremely well profit wise with the B&H with an AFN of 24.7 (+2,370% profit), but also equally as well for the two sell stop methods, 24.0 (2,400 % profit) for the 25% sell stop one, and even better 25.8 (2,480% profit) for the 10% sell stop method.

But the two sell stop methods (-23% max drawdown and -25% for 25% sell stop and 10% sell stop methods) out perform the B&H which cascades to -68% max loss.

Industrials

Moving on, the three methods perform very well for the industrials for the twenty year period. They profit about the same, ranging from 568% profit for the B&H, 500% for the 25% sell stop method, and 656% profit for the 10% sell stop one.

The methods diverge sharply on max drawdown, however. The B&H has the worst, at -61%, while the 25% sell stop and 10% sell stop methods clock in at -12% and -20%, collosal differences.

Some stark differences occur in individual stocks. For example, GE *loses* 88% with the B&H, while *gaining* 18% with the 10% sell stop method.

Boeing(BA) makes 245% profit when employing the B&H but considerably more using the 10% sell stop program, with 1,388% gained over the same period, while having a max loss in the portfolio of -18% versus -70% using the B&H.

ITW (Illinois Tool Works) does better when the B&H is used (+520%) versus that for the 10% sell stop method(+330%), but loses more on maximum drawdowns of -54% (B&H) versus -17% for the 10% sell stop regime.

Consumer Discretionary

The Consumer Discretionary sector has a wider range of results.

The overall ANF results are very good for all three strategies, and almost the same(1,400-plus % profits) for the 20 year period.

The trend in max drawdowns results continue, generally favoring the two sell stop strategies. The B&H shows an average of -72% max drawdowns, and the two stop methods do much better (-25% for the 25% sell stop and -31% for the 10% sell stop methods).

Individual stocks vary from poor results (Ford) to spectacularly successful ones like Amazon(AMZN). Ford lose 75% and Amazon gains 6,520 % with the B&H. Using the 25% and 10% sell stop techniques result in 70% gain and 17 % loss, respectively, for Ford. The two sell stop methods perform also spectacularly on AMZN, with 5,730% and 5,450 for 25% and 10% sell stop strategies.

Max drawdowns are much better with the two stop strategies for both stocks, losing no more than ½ that for the B&H strategy.

Nordstrom shows an extreme difference in returns and risk, for B&H (73% gain, -81 % max drawdown) versus the 10% sell stop program(1,210% gain, -6 % max drawdown).

Consumer Staples

There is a range in returns and risk(max drawdowns) in the consumer staples group, but not as pronounced as with other sectors. All three strategies show decent but not spectacular returns: ANFs of 3.42 (242% profit) for the B&H method, 2.77(177 % profit) for the 25% sell stop and 2.91(+191% profit) for the 10% sell stop method. But the max drawdown statistics are again much more favorable to the two sell stop methods(-16 % max drawdowns) versus -40% for the B&H, about a 2:1 ratio.

The contrast is classically shown with Walmart(WMT).

All three investment methods show pretty close AFNs: 2.52 for the B&H; 2.41 for the 25% sell stop approach, and the same for the 10% sell stop method. However, there is a sizable difference in max drawdown stats: -35% for the B&H; 0% for the 25% sell stop, and -13% for the 10% sell stop one.

Kroger(KR) is the only stock whose B&H is superior for both AFN results and max drawdown stats to the two sell stop methods, because the max drawdown numbers are fairly indistinguishable: -52 % for the B&H; and -32% and -41 % for the 25% and 10% sell stop strategies.

IT/Telecom

A mixed bag for IT/Telecom: 5 of the stocks do better with the two sell stop strategies, 5 do on balance the same(better/worse ANF, max drawdowns).

Over all the ANF for the B&H is 2.5, and 2.63 and 2.35 for the two sell stop strategies, a draw. However, the two sell stop methods are significantly better with max drawdowns of -37% and -35%, compared to -62 % for the B&H method.

Of the better ones, AT&T (T) embodies the total better ANFs of the two sell stop methods and max loss stats: the B&H *loses* -30% over the period, while the two sell stop methods lose -18%(25% sell stop) and *gain* 22%(10% sell stop method). The B&H has a maximum drawdown of -65% and the two sell stop methods have -25%(25 % sell stop) and -15%(10% sell stop method).

Similarly, HP Inc (HPQ) loses -42% for the B&H, and a loss of -26% for the 25% sell stop approach, but a *gain* of +185% for the 10% sell stop method. Max drawdown figures figures are -80% for the B&H, -50% and -20% for the two sell stop models, respectively.

On the negative side, Accenture (ACN) shows a +1,330% profit for the period for the B&H, and only +1,230% for the 25% sell stop model and +340% for the 10% mode. It is balanced, though by markedly better max drawdowns for the 25% method(0%) and 10% sell stop one(-14%) versus -46% for the B&H policy.

Another mixed bag is Qualcom(QCOM), which has a better ANF(3.03) for the B&H technique but better max drawdowns for the two sell stop techniques (-50% for the 25% sell stop, and -37% for the 10% sell stop) versus -68 % max drawdown for the B&H method.

Materials

The two sell stop techniques over all perform better than the B&H strategy in the materials sector, with a 5.54 recording for the 10% sell stop method, versus 4.03 for the B&H approach.

Both sell stop strategies outperform the B&H in max drawdown averages, with -42% and -30% worst drawdowns versus -73% for the B&H.

A spectacular example of the good use of a sell stop system is found with U.S. Steel (X). The buy-and-hold method *loses* -58% from 2000-2020, while the 25% sell stop and 10% sell stop strategies profit +507% and +650%, respectively. And both methods have far better max drawdowns, than the B&H (-97%!), coming with a third of the loss(-35%) and a fourth of the loss(-24%) for the 25% sell stop and 10% sell stop methods, respectively.

A truly mixed performance is recorded for FMC Corp.(FMC), where the B&H shows a great return of +1,020% for the period, but a respectable +611% profit for the 25% sell stop mode, and a superior +1,240% profit return for the 10% sell stop program.

Again, the two sells top programs do better than that for the B&H(-61%), recording for the 25% sell stop method (-54 %) drop maximum, and only -33% for the 10% sell stop one.

17

Utilities

The utilities sector has probably the most distinctly superior results for the ANF and max drawdown for the two sell stop strategies over the B&H, of all the sectors.

The B&H produces an over all average of +56% return for the period, versus +120% and +170% for the 25% sell stop and the 10% sell stop strategies.

Dramatic reductions in max drawdowns occur for the 25% sell stop (-26%) and the 10% sell stop (-18%), compared to a large number for the B&H (-70%) strategy over all utility stocks.

Two stock examples show marked contrast between the two sell stop methods and the B&H method: Duke Power(DUK) and Pacific Gas & Electric (PCG).

For DUK the B&H gains +22% over the period, while the two sell stop methods gain +82% for the 25% sell stop) and +92% (10% sell stop). Dramatic loss reduction is shown with only (0%) for the 25% sell stop approach and (-3%) for the 10% sell stop one. The B&H loses -71% max drawdown.

The most crushing comparison occurs with the performance of PCG, Unfortunately, the company ran into wildfire problems in California, and is suffering not only capital losses but also law suits. PCG managed to gain +54% for the period, but less than the 25% sell stop would have at +83%, and the 10% sell stop had profits of +147%.

The max drawdown also show a significant advantage for the 25% sell stop method(-39%) and the 10% sell stop technique (-35% versus a whopping -92% drop for the B&H approach.

Some Important Details

How do the investment trades look up close and personal? The following details give insight into the working of the sell stop-buy stop methods on a trade by trade basis, so you will better understand the workings and advantages of each method, be able to implement the strategies (see Chapter Five) and gain confidence in their use.

I will describe three indicie ETFs and 10 individual stocks traded, with results for the B&H and a sell stop strategy for each indicie and stock.

I will refer to tables explicitly detailing facts (purchase date, price paid, sell date, price received, profit/loss (P/L) of the trade, step aside months between current and the next trade, interest at a bank at that time, and Adjusted Nominal Fraction(ANF), starting at the beginning of the period at 1.0, and adjusted thereafter by gain/loss fractions and interest earned in the cash account after a trade, as a fraction of the portfolio current value).

The Indicies

First, let's examine the trading mechanics and efficacy of the B&H and a sell stop strategy on these three exchange ETFs (tradable Exchange Traded Funds, e.g. SPY for S&P 500 Index in Table 25)

<u>SPY</u>

For SPY the B&H and indeed the sell stop strategy starts on month end 2000/8(August 2000 at and ends at 308.5 on 2020/6. Mea culpa, I am reading from price and dates from charts (courtesy Charles Schwab, my broker) and you have to rely on my eyes and a sensitive mouse! See also Chart 3 for SPY prices. I use closing monthly prices to calculate entry/exit prices.

The buy-and-hold approach yields a return of +103% at the end of the 20 year period, a slightly less than average return per year return (about 5%), and over many years (100) of about 8%.

However, it suffers a maximum drawdown in early 2009 of -52% from a peak of about 155 in /10 to a low at 74. The 10% sell stop 33% buy stop retracement fraction (shown in Table 25) gets started at the same price as the B&H, at 152.3 on the 2000/8 close.

A sell stop is initially placed at 137.07, monthly. The sell stop is triggered on 2000/11 at 132, which we assume to be the transaction execution price. A loss of -13 % is recorded, and because we won't reenter the long position until a future buy stop is triggered on 2003/10, interest gathers on idle funds from the 2000/11 closing until reentry occurs after on the close of 2003/10, a span of 35 months, interest accrued of 9% (again, assuming an average of 3% annual interest, on all cash in indicie or stock accounts; yes, current rates are at best 1%, but past rates in the 1970s had risen to 10% or more, so this is an average, what I expect over all time, as an average interest rate).

The next (reentry) long position (we don't consider shorts, because of massive evidence of losing against over welming future economic and stock growth, and waiting for future positive short sell strategy research) is calculated as follows:

Wait for the (monthly) closing prices to continue to fall(maybe not!). We are anticipating the price drop so far (10% from the last top, when we placed the sell stop for the prior trade 10% below this last high) that prices will continue to drop and find a (final bottom or trough) that will produce a rise and favorable price for reentry to a long position.

Of course, we risk two miscalculations: not detecting the true(local) bottom before prices recover to yet new highs (new tops); and getting (sell) stopped out on the downs side towards the real bottom (premature buying, or on the upside from there, getting sell stopped (premature selling before, again, another bottom). Wheh! Prices during the entire drawdown/drop will test decisions made on sell *and* buy stops!

In this case, the second trade, reentry on 2001/5 is avoided because prices do not rise enough (to 126) against the rise requirement to trigger a long: suspected bottom at 117 (on 2001/3) plus 1/3 of (top 152-bottom 117) yielding 128 as a buy price specifies a price of 128 monthly closing or higher to trigger a reentry buy signal.

Further possible bottoms on 2001/9 and 2002/9 also do not trigger buy stop purchases, until a true (local) bottom occurs on 2003/9. The buy stop is then calculated as (top-bottom prices)times 1/3 (33%) plus the newly suspected bottom, or (152-82)x.333+ 82=105.3, which *does* occur at 106 on the close of 2003/10, where the investor purchases SPY at the market at that close or the next day at market (again we assume getting in on the morning following the triggered date at that price, even though practically the price execution will occur differently at slightly better or worse prices, or if the investor may try, a limit order at the triggered price. Either way I don't believe price executions *on average* will vary significantly from the triggered monthly closing price.

Transaction costs(commissions) are assumed to be zero, the current and expected future state. Even though we are looking at the past where commissions were small or substantial (the big, established brokerages), I assume the future is for minimal execution costs.

Subsequent trades occur like this: the long trade initiated on 2003/10 is stopped out on 2008/4 after surviving drawdowns of less than 10% from 2007/10 at about 155 until January 2008 closing of approximately 138. The trade is subsequently sell stopped out at 137.6 for a gain of 130%, and the account is further credited with interest earned for 19 months until the next (long) position is taken, resulting in the ANF on the account coming in at 1.345 times the previous ANF of 0.96(a first trade loss of 13% plus interest earned of 9%, equals a net of -4%, a resulting degradation of the initial ANF of 1.0 to 0.96).

And so subsequent purchases and sales and step asides result in successive trade values of +1%, +11%, +98%, and a -4% loss, and +8% on the final trade in the period, ending on 2020/6 (an open trade, so the trade is theoretically closed out). Notice that the prior trade, initiated on 2019/01, was sell stopped out on 2020/02 by a vicious downturn in the whole market, caused by the COVID-19 pandemic. Due to optimistic traders, the markets have since rebounded, resulting in a new long according to this sell stop/buy stop method, on 2020/03 at 290, and currently held.

The strategy results compare extremely well with the B&H policy. The 10% sell 33% buy stop reentry strategy beats the B&H by +418% profit return versus +103%, a resounding 4-fold better performance.

Also, very importantly, this sell stop/buy stop strategy, well outperformed the B&H on the risk front, with a showing a max drawdown of -4% versus a -52% drop for the B&H, a more than 10-fold improvement.

Caution: not all performance contrasts were that spectacular, as discussed further. But you get the idea: over all the sell stop-buy stop strategies out performed the B&H for 2 of three indicies, and the average of all stocks in the 9 S&P 500 sectors. And outperformed in maximum drawdowns for all indicies and stocks tested.

Moving on, Chart 4 depicts the Dow Industrials from 2000-2020. Table 26 shows the results of the 10% sell 33% buy stop method on the Dow ETF (DIA) for the period.

The buy -and -hold strategy shows a +124% return by the end of the period, with a maximum drawdown of about -50%, starting on on 2007/10 at 139, and ending on on 2009/02 at a bottom of 71(100x 139= 13,900 in cash nominal Dow value for the ETF).

The 10% sell stop 33% buy stop reentry program (Table 26) performs with a little less profits, +100%, but with a worst drawdown of -38%. So the comparison is a draw: more return (B&H) but more risk (also B&H).

Finally, the performances on the NASDAQ Composite ETF ($COMPX) will decide the superior strategy. See Chart 5 and Table 27 for the NASDAQ prices and 10% sell stop 33% buy stop strategy performances.

The B&H strategy gives a +140% profit return for the period, and a risk number, max drawdown, of -68%, occurring between 2007/01 at 3690 top and bottoming at 1170 on 20 12/09. So -so results, much risk, average returns.

The 10% sell and 33% buy stop strategy shows a return of +261% for the period, far superior to that for the B&H; and a worst drawdown of only -1%, infinitely desired, period, compared to the B&H's -68%.

Individual Stocks

<u>OXY</u> Moving on to individual stocks, let's look at a typical company in the oil sector, OXY. It has a long and storied history, and is one of the largest oil and gas exploration and production companies in the U.S.

Chart 6 depicts its price movements for the last two decades. It had a great run up from 12 to 112 in the first decade, and a sharp drop from that point on.

A buy-and-holder would have essentially broken even over 20 years, still showing a +70% gain at the 2020/06 close. However, its worst drawdown was -90%, devastating for the long termer, who is certainly anxious now and looking very carefully at the fundamentals of the company and industry, too.

If the investor had used the 10% sell stop 33% buy stop reentry system (Table 28), he/she would have fared far better: +662% gain for the period, and only -24% worst drawdown (from an ANF of 9.92 on 2011/06 to 7.62 on 2018/10)!

How did this happen? In hindsight, tight sell stops prevented large individual trade losses, and good reentry of long positions (remember, no shorts allowed!) provided large profit opportunities.

Reviewing the first few trades:

As always, we are assuming trading starts, as does the B&H policy, at the end of the period month beginning, here $10.8/share on 2000-07 closing (actually occurs the next trading day opening, but we'll assume for all strategies the execution of the trade results in a price equal to the closing price on the month's close that triggered a buy or sell stop).

The first long position is closed out on or after the close on 2001/06 at 13, after breaking a sell stop (mentally) placed at 13.5, resulting in a profit of +22%. Interest earned on idle after the trade is completed is for 6 months, or .015% until the next(long) is initiated.

The next long position occurs on of/after the 2001/12 closing at 13.32 after a 1/3 rebound from the latest low bottom of of 12.2 made on on 2001/9 from the top of 15.1 on 2001/04. The second trade is closed out on 2002/07 when prices drop 10% plus from another top at 15.1 on 2002/05, and a slight gain for the trade of +3% occurs.

The next trade begins on 2002/08 at 14.88 and runs unhindered/ no stop outs until 2016/10 sell stop closeout at 48.47, a +226% profit. And so on with generous profitable trades and small losses. Notice the account is protected at its peak on 2011/06 with subsequent but numerous small losses that add up to only -24%

BAC Moving to the financials, bank of America (BAC) represents the heart of U.S. having full service and scope of activities, from savings and loans to mortgage to investment banking.

For the 20 year period period it actually *lost* a smidgen, -10%, and had a worst drawdown of -93%, occurring in 2008-9 due to the financial crisis.

The 10% sell stop 33% buy stop program had an ANF of 2.23 or +123% profit, and far less maximum drawdown of -40%.

See Chart 7 for visual price presentation, and Table 29 for detailed trade information.

The first trade is initiated on the 2000/07 close at $26.90/share. A subsequent quick stop loss is executed on 2000/09 at 23.95, but the position is also reentered on the close of 2000/12 after rising over 1/3 of the drop from 2000/07 close from the 2000/11 bottom of 20.30 The first long position loses -11% but the second trade gains +28%. The worst drawdown occurs on 2011/04 after several small to moderate losses in a row. The drawdowns average -27% overall. But a nice method performance over all, snatching victory from the jaws of defeat with moderate losses.

UNH

The next example is from a very successful sector, the health industry. United Healthcare (UNH) is a prominent health services company with many millions of customers.

See Chart 8 for visuals and Table 30 for the 10% sell stop 33% buy stop strategy results.

Who wouldn't include this gem in their portfolio? If bought and held for the 20 year span 2000-2020, the investor would have have gained a whopping +2,370 % gain, but accompanied by a large max drawdown of -68% from the beginning of 2006 to nearly 2014, bottoming before on 2009/02.

Believe it or not, the 10% sell stop 33% buy stop program actually outperformed the buy-and-hold one, in both profits (+2,486%) and markedly in maximum drawdown (-18%).

Referring to Table 30, the first trade is closed out after a monthly close of 14.4 on 2001/06 triggers a sell stop. The very next month trading resumes (on/after a 2001/07 close of 15.2) Yes, you can execute on the close of 2001/07 if you have calculated the buy stop (and also the sell stop on the new position) ahead of time (See Chapter Five for detailed calculating procedures and operational rules).

The third trade is entered on 2006/12 close when prices rise more than 33% from the stock price drawdown, starting at 62.3 on 2005/12 and bottoming at 43.8 on 2006/05. But the trade is quickly stopped out on 2007/09, the beginning of the financial bust.

Another trade is initiated again quickly on 2007/10 close, but even quicker stopped out at 50.5 on 2008/01. A series of little losses occur but then a mighty price uptrend takes hold thereafter(position entry begins on 2010/06 at 30.6, and ends on 2018/12 with a huge price increase to 248.25).

BA

For the industrial sector, I chose Boeing (BA), for it well represents a solid industry, commercial aircraft production, and also military products.

See Chart 9 for pictorials and Table 31 for the fine details of using the 10% sell stop 33% buy stop strategy. If you bought and held BA for the whole 20 years, you would have achieved a good return of +245%, albeit with a hefty maximum drawdown (late 2007 top-early 2009 bottom) of -70%.

The 10% sell stop 33% buy stop method would have returned *more* for the investor's account(+1,388%), while only suffering a -18% maximum dreawdown, from 2015/08 to 2016/01.

It doesn't show show on the chart, but the first trade is initiated on 2000/07 at 53.6 and closed out on 2001/01, at 59 on 2001/01 due to a drop in price triggering a sell stop from a 2000/11 closing of 69.6, the top of the current price move.

The position is immediately reentered the next month's closing(2001/02) at 62.5, closed out again with a quick sell stop execution at 56 on 2001/06. One more stop out occurs for a loss of 7% on 2002/05, then a strong upwards movement results in a fourth trade of 180%.

AMZN

We now turn to the consumer discretionary industry.

Amazon, the legendary online retailer, has a penchant for reinvestment of its behemouth revenue and paying little if any dividends- *expanding forever*, its motto. Its profits and price continue to skyrocket, year in and year out. See chart 10 for price display 2000-2020.

A long term holder would have received a huge payout, +6,520% for the period 2000-2020, but with very large drawdown in 2000-2003 of -86%. Wouldn't it be nice if he could capture that gain without the unnerving drop?

Yes, he could if were willing to give up a little of the monster gain in exchange for a significant, sizable reduction of risk.

The 10% sell stop 33 % buy stop reentry system (see Table 32 for trade results) generated a little less profits(+5,450%), but cut risk or maximum drawdown by more than half, to -42%. The loss period occurred in a sideways, meandering market, when prices whipsawed back and forth by varying on the upside and downside by 10%, a sensitive whipsaw range for this strategy. Sort of like the Washington State bridge Gallopin Gertie that undulated in 1940 due to wind and construction problems.

The trading starts with two losses related to the 2000-2003 tech bust, with a cumulative/ compound loss of -20%, but swiftly gets back on track with the general price rise from 2003-2004, falls flat with bridge/market vibrations in 2004-2006, but then soars upwards with the climbing price movement of 2007-2020, despite a general price drawdown in 2008-2009 of -50%.

CLX

The consumer staples industry is a steady but unspectacular one, with a few good standouts and many mediocre performances. Its main appeal is steadiness: small share price drawdowns.

Clorox is a good example. The company has a wide range of basic consumer products, household cleaning, grocery and specialty food items, and personal care products.

Its ANF for the period was 6.01 or +501% net profit, a very sound return for the B&H policy, with only a maximum drawdown of -30%. Look at Chart 11 to see the price steadiness!

The 10%sell 33% buy stop program did well, too (+325%), just not as good. Its max drawdown was stingy, though at -11% a 2/3 drop from the B&H max drawdown of -30%. In fact the losses were tiny- 10%,-7%,-3% and -5%.

ACN

The technology and telecommunications industries had the most wide range of returns and risk, but rather average, sub-par returns, over the period 2000-2020. Some yielded spectacular return results, like Apple in the +6,000% area, but also firms that *lost* money (AT&T -30%, CISCO -32%). As a whole the industry here in this sample of 10 companies averaged +150% in profit, but with a -62% average max drawdown.

Outstanding returns were made by Accenture (ACN), at +1,330%, with a relatively moderate maximum drawdown of -46%. See Chart 12 for a very steady uphill climb in share prices all along, despite early bumps in the 2000-2003 era and again in 2008-2009.

The 10% sell 33% buy stop method (see Table 33 for trading results) performs well in returns(+313%), but nowhere near the stellar performance of the B&H. It made up for that in sharply better max drawdown of -14% due to two trades in the 2008-2009 financial bust.

ORCL

On the other end of the tech industry spectrum Oracle (ORCL) continued to puzzle investors with a disappointing return of +23% over 20 years. It also had a bad maximum drawdown of -82% using the B&H method.

The firm concentrates on database management systems business applications. & buy stop strategy results. Refer to Chart 13 for a price chart of the period, and Table 35 for the 10% sell 33% buy stop strategy results.

The returns were far better, at +163%, and a maximum drawdown was only -22%, a ¾ reduction compared to -82% for the B&H strategy. Its only significant loss loss occurred on 2011/12 when the method lost -22% in a trade. Even though prices plunged from 2000/07 at around 40 to a bottom in mid 2002 of around 8, this strategy quickly exited the long position at 45.1 in 2000/08, and never reentered until 2007/05 at 20 when prices were starting to rise significantly. A whipsaw market accounted for a -22 % loss on 2011/12.

X

The materials sector has both a wide range of material production, from steel to mining to wood products, and a similar wide range of returns and risks.

U.S. Steel (X) unfortunately symbolizes the bottom rung, showing for the B&H investor a *loss* for the 20 year period of -58%, and a catastrophic max drawdown of -97%, driving most investors crazy.

Chart 14 and Tale 36 display this miserable performance.

However, strategy #3 the 10% sell and 33% buy stop strategy, turns these results right around despite and due to some cycles of rising prices between drops (see Chart 14, a huge rise from 10 to 185 in the period 2003-2008, but followed by a vicious drop back down to 20 and interminable back and forth price movements with sizable drops in 2012, 2016, and finally another hard drop from 50 to 7 in 2018-2020.

The 10% sell 33% buy stop method, after a few minor losses, racks up steady gains that eventually propel the account to +650% overall gains with only a -24% worst drawdown, in *sharp* contrast to the B&H technique.

<u>PCG</u>

The utilities sector represent the moderate growth(for most) companies that are public service energy providers, known for steady dividends, but not unbeknown to most investors, rather burdened with risk as measured by maximum and average drawdowns. The industry had only a modest over all gain average of +56%, but with an attendant -70% average max drawdown, not a good profit/ risk ratio.

Pacific Gas & Electric (PCG) took low honors with a -70% loss and a -92% max drawdown for the buy-and-hold strategy.

Look to Chart 15 for visuals and Table 37 for the results of the 10% sell and 33% buy stop strategy for this stock.

First of all, the price behavior was extreme: huge jagged ups and downs during the 2000-2008 market bubbles, then a fast-pounding move from 12 to 72 until 2018, when it fell precipitously due to wild fires and company culpability for the fires.

Normally large pension funds and institutions would invest heavily in this type of utility for sure and steady results. Not here! This proves the real necessity of risk management, yet yielding some decent returns!

The 10% sell 33% buy stop approach comes to the rescue here. With stringent sell stop protection (for 2000-2003), and buy stop opportunities when price rises occur(2003-2008), the strategy resulted in +170% over all gain for the period, and only -35% maximum drawdown.

Some Reflections: Conclusions on Uses

Over all, the two sell stop/buy stop systems seem to significantly improve on results for the indicie ETFs and some more for stock sectors and individual stocks via larger profits/returns and significantly on maximum drawdown for everything tested.

Personal or institutional use for any of these systems depend upon one's own risk/return profile:

Buy-and-hold users should expect great returns (depending upon good stock selection) and can stand virtually any risk(drawdowns/price retreats); moderate risk investors might choose the 25% sell stop 33% buy stop reentry strategy; and those most risk adverse should choose the 10% sell 33% buy stop plan (although many times better returns can also be obtained with this method, like having cake and eating it, too).

There is a wide range of returns (and risks, often tied to returns) between sectors and individual stocks. With poorly performing stocks, either because of industry pressures/conditions on individual circumstances (management, e.g.) return performances can be greatly limited, and investors should stay away.

Greatly performing stocks (Amazon, Apple, Tesla, e.g.) naturally lend themselves to the three strategies, but must be tamed with risk reduction surety by using the sell stop/buy stop strategies. Instead of -50%, -70%, or even occasionally _90% drawdowns devastating to the portfolio in fact and psychologically, it is much better to use the large risk reduction capability of the stop strategies, even if reducing somewhat returns.

It certainly also points to the need for good stock/indicie selection in the first place! See <u>Chapter Six</u> on selection advice.

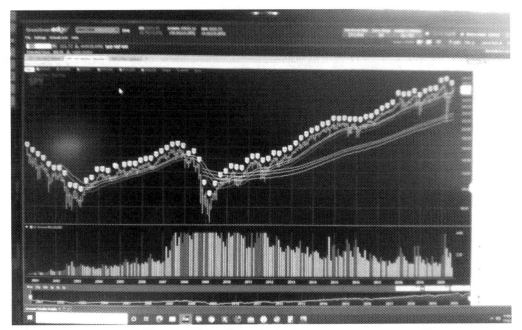

Chart 3 SPY

Chart 5 $COMPX monthly

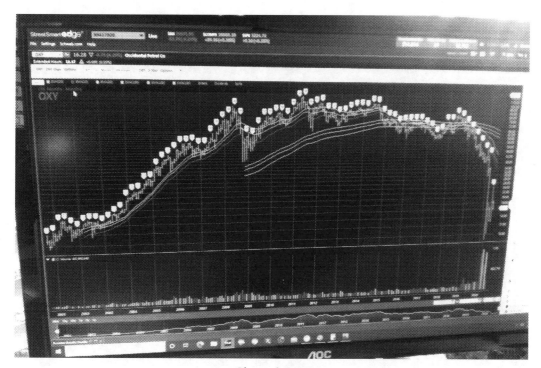

Chart 6 OXY

Chart 7 BAC

Chart 9 BA Monthly

Chart 10 AMZN

Chart 11 CLX

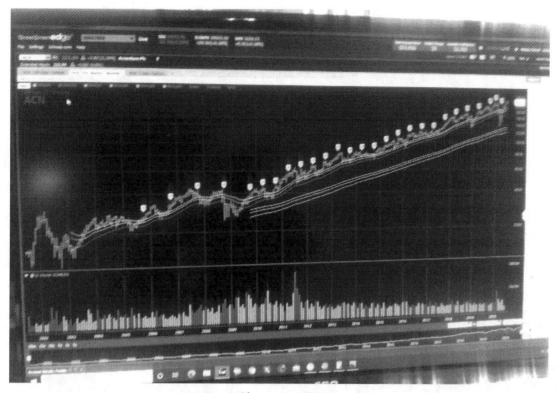

Chart 12 ACN

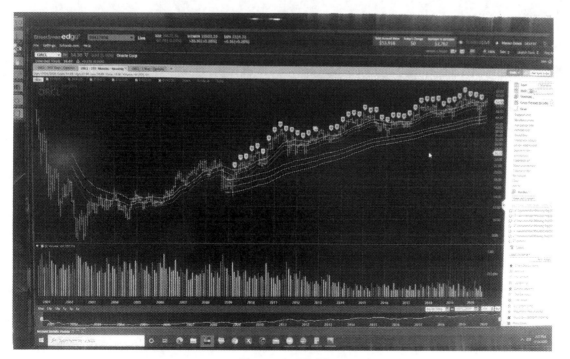

Chart 13 ORCL

Chart 14 X

CHAPTER FIVE

Practical Investment Plans

A quick recap on the theory behind stop use for the portfolio: sell stops can be thoughtfully constructed to *limit losses* (both individually and cumulatively); and buy stops can be judiciously calculated to discover when to reenter the long term uptrend. Chapter Four did some detailed tests on market index ETFs and individual stocks to demonstrate usefulness. Indeed, profits were better and losses (and especially max drawdowns) were strongly reduced for the two stop methods compared to the buy-and-hold strategy.

The stop strategies can be used by long term investors to *sharply* reduce losses(open or closed out), but still hold onto or improve total portfolio gains, while short term traders can build up substantial gains to rival the buy and hold approach, still keeping portfolio drawdowns small.

Now it comes down to crafting plans for individual and institutional investors.

The strategy choices for using index ETFs or individual stocks:

The choices range from (1) buy-and -hold (possibly huge gains, but certainly huge ongoing paper losses); (2) the 25% sell stop 33% buy stop method (much of long term gains, good protection on losses); and(3) the 10% sell stop 33% buy stop method (moderate to large profits, small losses). The following steps must be taken first and ongoing: picking the method best for your profile; employing discipline for the method chosen; side items, like interest taken on idle funds; withdrawl of funds policy; and of course implementing the actual details for using each plan.

Pick The Best Plan For You

Choosing the right plan for you involves two major factors: selection of portfolio items (individual stocks, ETFs, or other media like futures, currencies, fixed income, etc.); and management of the items (entry and exit policies, e.g.). Chapter Six discusses selection.

The first step is to determine your return/risk profile. And continue to review it, as time, your physical and mental health, and other circumstances (job or family change, corporate reorganization, e.g.) may significantly change.

You must be frank about the review. Your sticking to the plan and comfort with portfolio performance depends on it.

Do you want huge profits and can accept lots of risk(large paper losses, i.e.)? Or do you require/

need very strict/small risk (loss) control, and will accept small/smaller returns in return for tight loss control. Or some combination in between – moderate risk control (say, 25% maximum drawdowns) and moderate returns (*% per year, say).

Of course, some investors dream of huge profits with minimal risk. Guess what: that's not probably going to happen. Size of return and risk go hand in hand.

If you can stand great risk in return for huge profit potential, then choose the buy-and-hold plan.

If you determine you are mid-to-moderate return-risk investor (can stand 25% drawdowns or slightly larger, and desire 8% or larger return average), then pick the 25% sell 33% buy stop strategy.

Or, if you can stand small to moderate risk in return for above average returns(8%, say, competitive with interest bearing accounts-but not *now*!), then the 10% sell 33 % buy stop strategy is you cup of tea.

Discipline/Expectations

Once you've determined your real investment profile and chosen the appropriate investment plan, you must stick to it, through thick and thin, otherwise the plan won't perform well. (No management overrides!).

This point is obvious, but it isn't the ability and conviction on the part of the investor to strictly follow both the meaning and letter of the plan:

If you are using the buy-and-hold strategy: if a large loss, say of 60% (on paper) happens, you must not abandon the project just because you don't like it, or didn't expect it (after all black swan, improbable events do occur, and are often unseen or unpredictable, but that's life).

If you are using the 10% sell stop 33% buy stop system and losses mount to -25% and you planned on only 10-15% drawdowns, you should take your lumps. Your estimates are based on prior markets, and there is no guaranty or good reason to expect exactly the same gains and losses to repeat. Most likely there is an industry or macroeconomic reason for the current downdraft in prices, affecting all stocks. If there is, live with it until conditions return to (nearly) normal and you get the expected performance.

If not, conduct a quant test by calculating the average and standard deviation of the past 24 months returns. Then subtract 3 times the standard deviation number from the average return. If this difference is smaller than or about the same as this month's return, then ignore the current month's performance.

Example: if the average monthly return of a stock is +0.80%, the standard deviation is 3.0%, then the critical number to examine is 0.80-3x 3.0=--8.2%. If the current monthly performance is -6.0%, this is above the critical number and the investor should (regrettably, but) ignore this monthly performanc.

If the difference is more (here, say, -10.5 %) then he should consider reviewing and replacing, for fundamental reasons, the stock/indicie picked for the portfolio. Add stronger (return-wise or risk-wise) stocks. Delete significantly long-term losers.

Also, you may upgrade to the next higher risk plan, the 25% sell stop 33% buy stop strategy, or the buy-and-hold if you now can stand the increased risk.

Interest On Idle Funds

If you use the buy-and-hold strategy, you won't have the opportunity to earn interest on your (fully invested) account.

On the other hand, if the investor uses one of the sell-buy stop strategies, he/she can make interest on idle funds, when no trades are in place, for each stock or ETF. Periods of idle funds (no trades occurring) can range from 1-2 months to years, and (when the interest rates count) that can mean significant returns added to profits/losses after completed trades. Be ready to write/transfer to your bank/interest bearing institution for excess funds available the minute the trade is finished and funds are available. And be ready to replace those funds back into your trade account the minute you need to have available funds to reenter trades.

Withdrawls

Generally, withdrawls are verboten, not allowed. The purpose of the plans is to build wealth, as constant goal, for your retirement or grave emergencies, or for clients if you are an institution.

If you do need cash for an emegency, death or client redemption, then do it as follows: divide the withdrawl amount by 12, liquidate 8.5% of that amount each month (sell 8.5% of the amount needed held in stocks/indicies each month, evenly). Foe example, if $100,000 in cash is needed, $8500 of stock is evenly sold over all item in the portfolio, and placed in cash for account/accrual/dispersion or redemption each month.

The rational behind this procedure is that the position reduction is averaged /leveled off over time to accommodate (mimic) the portfolio's medium term performance, and not jeopardize and adversely affect the immediate/short term results.

Implementing The Three Plans

Implementing/using these three strategies (buy-and-hold; 25% sell 33% buy stop; and 10% sell 33% buy stop strategies) is broken down into two situations: initial (beginning) the strategy; and continuing trading the strategy.

All the instructions below pertain to the monthly closings of the stock or ETF under question.

<u>Initial Entry</u>

<u>B&H</u>

For the buy-and-hold strategy, there are two practical/ available choices: (1) buy the amount allocated to the stock in question (most advisors suggest suggest equal amounts per stock because we don't know/expect projected stocks' performance, i.e. we're unbiased), at the market (recommended).

Or (2) choose a time (still buy at market) or price you deem is possible. Here you are guessing what time/price combination is good/possible and will occur; not really based on solid information. Not recommended. Smacks of of too much judgment or greed> The B&H really assumes we do not know future prices and that and that the buy-and-hold does best over intermediate and long term.

<u>Initial Entry</u>
<u>(Sell Stop</u>
<u>Buy Stop</u>
<u>Strategies)</u>

For both stop strategies, the investor should buy at the market on the first monthly close

The investor now places a (mental) stop X% below the first monthly closing price, and marks that price in his notebook, and also stipulates in his notebook that the fist monthly closing to be the first top T and first bottom B (to be referred to in "ongoing calculations", next). Here X% is equal to 25% for the 25% sell stop 33% buy stop approach, and 10% for the 10% sell stop 33% buy stop strategy.

So the initial long position is the current monthly closing price, the sell stop is (mentally) placed X% (25% for one strategy, 10% for the other one) below the long position entry price, and the current top T and bottom B are also set to be equal to the current monthly closing price.

<u>Ongoing B&H</u>
<u>Calculations</u>

There are no ongoing calculations for this method, because we are holding the position for the entire period.

<u>Ongoing Calculations/Actions</u>
<u>Sell Stop/Buy Stop</u>
<u>Methods</u>

After the first position is taken, new top and bottom calculations are needed and are made, and actions taken, at each new monthly closings as follows:
<u>Calculations</u>
Higher close (current monthly close price is *higher* than the current topT)
Reset current top T to be the current monthly closing price, and record it in notebook
Lower close(current monthly close is *lower* than last monthly close price)
Reset current bottom B to be equal to the current monthly close price, record in notebook

Next, determine what to do with your new top and bottom resets:
<u>Actions</u>
If currently **long**, check if current monthly closing price is *lower* than current sell stop price

      NO -   no action: wait for next monthly close.

      YES –   close out long position at market, on current monthly close or immediately next morning

      YES –   note *no* current position in notebook

      YES -   designate new bottom B will be equal to current monthly closing price, and calculate new buy stop price for new long as equal to: the new bottom B plus buy stop fraction (in both stop strategies here equal to .333 or 33 1/3%) times (current top T -current bottom B).

If currently *no* long position is held,

    (a) update current top T:

> If current monthly closing price is *lower/equal* to current top T then *no* top recalculation is needed
>
> If current monthly closing price is *higher* than the current top T, make top T to be equal to the current monthly closing price, and note in notebook.

    (b) update current bottom B:

> If current monthly closing price is *higher than/equal to* current bottom B, then no bottom update is needed.
>
> If current monthly closing price is *lower* than current bottom bottom B, make current bottom B equal to the current monthly closing price, and note in notebook

    (c) check for *new* long position:

> If current monthly closing price is *higher* than the current buy stop price, then take/execute *new* long position at the market on the monthly close or immediately the next morning, and note new position in notebook.
>
> If current monthly closing price is *lower* than the current bottom B
>
>   NO- no new calculations are needed
>
>   YES – Set new bottom B equal to current monthly closing price
>
> YES – Calculate new buy stop price and record in notebook:
>
> *new buy stop price* = new bottom B plus buy stop fraction times (current top-new bottom B). For our methods here the buy stop fraction is .333

Let's do some examples:

Example (1) S&P 500 (SPY)

Refer to Chart 3, and Table 25 S&P 500 results for the 10% sell stop 33% buy stop strategy.

The first long position is taken on the first monthly closing, shown, 2000/08 at 152.3, becoming the position price.

The top T is set at 152.3, bottom B at 152.3, and sell stop set at at 10% below the position price, at 137.07

The next monthly (2000/09) closing price (145.9) is less than the previous closing of 152.3, and thus is tested for a sell stop execution (sell stop is not violated) and there is an updating of bottom B price to 145.7, noted in our notebook(for future reference).

The following month, 2000/10 closing is slightly lower (143.9, but not breaking the sell stop price, but again lowering the bottom B to 143.9, and noted in our notebook.

Finally, on 2000/11, the monthly closing price of 132 breaks the sell stop of 137.07, and so thew position is closed, no position is now in effect, a new bottom B is set to 132, all noted in the notebook.

We now search for reentry to a long position.

The next month's closing price is close to that for 2000/11, so no action or T/B recalculations are needed.

On 2001/01, there is a rise in monthly closing price to approximately 137.6, so a test for a buy stop trigger is made. The new buy stop price (figured on 2000/12) is 132+.333x(152.3-132)= 138.8, not quite as low as 137.6, the current monthly closing price, so no action is taken and no updates made (top T still stands at 152.3, bottom B = 132.).

On 2001/02 monthly closing prices drop to 124, still signaling no buy, but a new bottom B of 124 is set, and a new buy stop price is set equal to 124+.333x(152.3-124)=133.4 and noted for action next month in the notebook.

Another drop on 2001/03 to 117.3 drops the bottom B to 117.3 and recalculates a new buy stop price to 117.3+.333x(152.3-117.3)=128.9.

The next month's closing price rises to 127.6, but doesn't quite trigger a buy. No actions or T/B updates, so on to the next monthly closing price.

Prices continue to drop, new bottoms are made, on 2001/08 and 2001/09, and another test of a buy stop price = 105.5 (the bottom on 2001/09)+.333x(152.3-105.5) = 121.1 isn't met at the next month's closing on 2001/10 of 114.9

Finally, a (final) bottom on 2002/09 at 82.2 occurs, and the new buy stop price is calculated as 82.2+.333x(152.3-82.2) =105.5, which isn't met until the 2003/10 monthly closing, so a new long position is established then(2003/12 closing) at 106, and a sell stop is placed at 106x.90=95.4.

The sell stop is not henceforth violated(triggered) even when raised after new high monthly closings, until 2008/01 when the sell stop at 139.23 is triggered at the monthly closing of 137.6, the position is closed and set to zero, a new low is set and bottom B designated, a new top T set to 155.7(from 2007/10 monthly closing), all recorded in the notebook.

Example (2)
Occidental Petroleum
OXY)

Follow on Chart 6 and Table 28, results for the 10% sell stop 33% buy stop strategy.

We take the first long position on the monthly close of 2000/07 at 10.8.

Per instructions for the initial trade entry date, we buy at the market at the end of the month closing of 2000/07, place a sell stop at 10% below the entry price, or at 9.8 and set the first top T at 10.8 and first bottom B also at 10.8., and record these settings in the notebook.

We then check the next month's closing price(for 2000/08) to see if the position is closed out and if top T or bottom B is adjusted.

Indeed, the next month closes the same at 10.8 so we can move on and leave the sell stop unchanged and wait for the next month's closing (No changes in top T or bottom B either).

The close of 2000/10 is close, but we escape the sell stop triggering. And we raise the new top T to that closing price, and note so in the notebook.

The monthly closing prices keep rising, and we continue to raise the sell stop price, finally on 2000/12 a monthly close of 12.2 makes us place a sell stop at 11.0 for the 2001/01 close, but it closes at 11.3, and we again escape execution of the sell stop.

Finally on 2001/04 the monthly closing price rises to 15.1 so we place a mental sell stop at 13.6, which is executed on 2001/06 monthly close at 13.4 at which point we close out the long position for a +22% profit. We set the position to zero, the new bottom to 13.4, and record these facts in the notebook.

From here we are looking to get back in the long position, waiting for a bottom and a significant rise from the bottom to the old top of at least 33 1/3%, to trigger a reentry to the long position.

A rise the next month and succeeding months goes up to 13.7. Is it enough to signal a buy? Calculating the buy stop trigger price, is equal to the current bottom 13.4 on 2001/06 plus 33 1/3 % of top T to bottom B (15.1-13.4) = 14.0. Not quite: the next monthly close is 13.9(whew, close!)

On 2001/09 monthly closing prices drop to 12.23, and a new buy stop price is calculated, as the new bottom B becomes 12.23, to equal to 12.23+.333x(15.2-12.23) = 13.23.

The next monthly closing (2001/12) of 13.32 triggers a reentry long position. The initial sell stop is placed (mentally) at 90% of 13.32, or 12.0, and (initially) bottom B at 13.32 also. The position is set to long, and current top T set to the current monthly closing price, and these changes are noted in the notebook(always!).

The next month, 2002/01, a small decrease in monthly closing price does not trigger a sell stop, so we move on to successive rising monthly close prices, except for one small decrease on 2002/04, which also does not trigger a sell stop.

Finally, prices close at 15.1 on 2002/05 and a sell stop is set at .90x15.1=13.73 for 2002/06 and the succeeding month, which does trigger a sell out of the position, for a +3% small profit. The position counter is set to zero(none), new bottom is set to 13.73

And so on.

Example (3)
Pacific Gas & Electrical
(PCG)

See Chart 15 and Table 37.

The first long, as always, is taken at the first monthly closing price, 2000/07 at 29.2 The initial sell stop is set at (90%) of 29.2, or 26.3. The initial bottom B and top T are also set to 29.2, and recorded in the notebook.

The very next monthly closing on 2000/08 is 24.2, triggering the sell stop and position exit at that price. The current position is made zero, and new bottom is also set to 24.2 and recorded in the notebook. The position is closed for a -17% loss.

The next buy stop price is quickly calculated to be new bottom B+.333x(current top T-bottom B)=25.86, and is quickly filled at 26.9 on 2000/09 monthly closing.

The position is set to "on", or 1. The current top T is set to 26.9. The sell stop is calculated at .9x26.9 =24.2 for the next monthly close price, all recorded in the notebook.

Unfortunately, the next monthly closing price falls on 2001/1 to 20.1, hugely breaking the sell stop at 24.2. A loss of -25% is booked, slightly mitigated by interest earnings 2%, keeping the drawdown at that point to -35%, which happens to be the worst drawdown the system will endure in the 20 years traded.

Prices proceed to fall all the way to 9.1 on 2001/04, but a rapid recovery starts after that date.

On 2001/04 closing a buy stop price reentry long is calculated as the current bottom B (having been lowered dramatically from 2000/11 at 20.4 to 9.1 on 2001/04, to 9.1) +(.333x(current top T-current bottom B) or (27.5—9.1) = 9.1 + .333x18.6=15.2.

Eventually, on 2001/08 this buy stop is executed, at 16.4. A sell stop is set at 0.9x16.4=14.6, and revised repeated with higher monthly closes until a peak on 2002/03 at 26.3. The sell stop is then set at .90x26.3= 23.67

Prices sharply drop to 18.1 on 2002/06. The position is closed, new bottom B set at 18.1, with the top T remains at 23.6, recorded in the notebook, and we are waiting for a new bottom(or not) and rise to trigger a reentry long. The trade yields a +10% profit.

Prices again fall dramatically, making the investor keep setting lower bottoms B until on 2002/10 a new bottom B becomes 10.8, and buy stop reentry price is calculated as the current bottom +.333x(current top T– current bottom B)= 10.8+.333x(23.6-10.8) = 15.1 which is executed on 2003/04.

The position is held for a long time, until 2007/06, and sold for a +198% profit. The strategy survived drawdowns and prospered in big whipsaw markets.

Implement Plans Summary

The specifics of the plan have just been enumerated. Here's a quick summary,.

(1) <u>Choose Plan</u>
Pick the strategy that best suits your profile or situations
Choose stocks/indicie ETFs to trade.
Assign (equal?) monies to each stock/indicie

(2) Initiate (long) position
For all strategies, the simplest and recommended procedure is to buy at the market at the end of the month

(3) Ongoing trade management (all at monthly closings):
For the buy-and– hold technique, do nothing but hold the (long) position.

For the two sell stop-buy stop strategies:
      (a) Check for new tops T or bottoms B, calculate any new buy stop price and
          log changes in notebook.
      (b) Actions:
          If long, test for trigger of sell stop:
               No- then no further action
               Yes- close out position, reset position counter to zero, designate
                    new bottom B, calculate new buy stop price, record these in
                    notebook.

If no position, check current monthly closing to see if buy stop price is
triggered

> No - then no further action

> Yes – reenter long position, calculate new sell stop, set position
> counter to "1" or "on", set new top T, and record these changes
> in notebook.

Summary

In summary, the sell stop - buy stop strategies employ long positions only and limit losses by
setting close sell stops, and improve profits by setting buy stops to enter often early on price rebounds.
Over all, it produces stronger growth and much less losses or drawdowns, than the buy-and-hold
philosophy.

CHAPTER SIX

Stocks Selection And Future Research

The results of the three investment strategies (buy-and-hold and two sell stop-buy stop strategies are substantive, giving the investor or institution very good result possibilities.

But performance, both profit and risk, can be improved. The buy-and-hold yields approximately 8% per year long term, but suffers from large and prolonged drawdowns or drops in value. Even though the two stop strategies dramatically improve risk(by almost 100%, or 50% reduction) upon the buy-and-hold method, it only over all moderately kicks up portfolio returns (although for some stocks and indicies the improvement is very significantly larger).

In particular, markedly larger returns are found in 4 of 9 S&P 500 sectors; essentially the same in two sectors; and less so in two others, for the stop loss - buy stop strategies, compared to the buy-and-hold one. Over all sectors the 25% sell stop strategy does a little better, and the 10% sell stop marks a considerable improvement over the B&H method.

But both stop strategies greatly outshine the buy-and-hold when it comes to risk control, as measured by maximum drawdown; -67% average max drawdown for the B&H; far less, about -25%, for the two stop strategies.

How about improving both return and risk performances with *better* stock selection?

Many investors, money managers, and analysts do indeed take that step, with mixed results. (See Chapter Two for a detailed discussion).

The basic premise for those adhering to 'fundamental' approach is that using company and industry information such as price history, book value, cash flow, revenue, earnings, dividends, and hybrid statistics like price/earnings ratios, operating income, depreciation, expenses, taxes, and balance sheet information about assets and liabilities to arrive at conclusions about profitability and risk for the firm in question will yield good selection.

Conclusions and recommendations range from specific findings about future revenues, profit margins, acquisitions, and management actions (like personnel and expansions), investment plans and industry fortunes and outcomes constitute many forecasts. Assumptions and caveats are also enumerated.

Most critical factors, I believe, are the company's particular dynamics (its industry outlook, its management team, cash and indebtedness, revenues and earnings). Down to two essentials, I think most depends upon the industry's outlook and the company's management. The rest (earnings, cash indebtedness, etc.) follows from these two items.

Another peeve I have is that management must use technology more and more, especially management science methods, including improved mathematical forecasts and data management ones.

In sum, I would argue that investors/managers should emphasize strong growth industries, such as currently health, tech and perhaps financial(simply because it is often at the forefront and heavily involved in the lifeblood: money needs).

But we also need imaginative management thinking: forward looking (new products/ industries, e.g.). Obviously Steve Jobs and Apple, Bill Gates and Microsoft(breakthrough products/new software), and recently Elon Musk (autos and space innovation).

Management (including boards of directors) reviews should be conducted more often, to constantly monitor all aspects of the company: revenue sources(advertising, e.g.); personal performances/turnover reviews; expenses; industry changes; product status;tax changes; and more.

Also, more and more emphasis on analytical techniques should take place, like quantitative forecasting and other management methods (inventory and customer modeling, for instance). Over all, better management decision (science) techniques should be introduced and relied upon.

Future Research

Better stock selection will undoubtedly help the portfolio, but what else can the investor/ manager do?

Generally, we should encourage imaginative approaches to investment management: innovative insight into industry change and new industry recognition and fostering; new or improved management science applications to investment research, like improving forecasting methods.

For the three strategies studied in this book, here are some ideas:

Buy and Hold Strategy

Besides better stock selection (stay away from old stodgy ones, like railroads, steel, and perhaps GE and PCG, and maybe old coal utility firms), but *do* select/ concentrate on excellent new industry prospects(high tech, advanced health, brand new concept industries).

We should think about improvements in initial position entry and further points if you have more cash now available: based on drawdown dynamics, for instance, sensitive interim top and bottom detection techniques, for example.

Stop Strategies

Everything can be improved.

The sell stop buy stop strategies explained in this book have shown dramatic risk reduction and decent if not better returns than the buy-and-hold method.

Some possible improvements:

Sell/Buy Stop Percentages

I tested several percentages, ranging from 10% to 25% for sell stops and 20% to 67% for buy stop reentry fractions on the latest top T and bottom B differences, to add to the latest bottom to get a but stop price on the month's closing price.

I found that a middle area of 10%-25% for sell stop percentages worked well, but numbers below (5%) and above(50%) were too close to results of the buy-and-hold method, or to close to tiny price moves, making for many whipsaw losses adding up to too much account value degradation.

On buy stop percentages, I also found too early reentry (20 % fraction or lower) tripped off too many sell stop losses, and too large (67%) provided too large a difference between prior exit prices and the (higher) reentry from the larger buy stop reentry fraction, hence leading to smaller eventual reentry gains.

So in the future we can test refinements, other values between the 10-30% for sell stops, and 25-50% for buy stop settings.

The levels of testing might change for different top and bottom designations (local tops, bottoms?), and stops (especially buy stops) could be set to price levels, not percent retracements of the top of the top-bottom drop. Different definitions of tops and bottoms themselves might prove interesting.

Dynamic modeling might find patterns reliably defining tops and bottoms (see the price vector model in my book Trading Systems Analysis)

Also, account management might dictate patterns in gains/losses, indicating when over all to stop/restart trading. For example, it might help to initiate actual trading after the first trade, which tends to be a loser; or again patterns/general market analysis that suggests avoidance or double-up or more on specific trades.

Different Media

Other media, from stock options to futures, and options, currencies, and fixed income, could be lucrative areas for the two stop strategies.

Stock options, of course, are stock price-based, and will act like stocks, only much more highly leveraged.

Futures present a similar situation to stock options in terms of leverage, but of course represent a wholly, large, different subject matter, from agriculture to hard and soft commodities(sugar, cocoa, coffee, orange juice, milk) to medals to financial subjects (bonds, T-bills, notes), and currencies.

Fixed income represents the debt markets, contracted interest returns on government and corporate borrowings.

Quant Techniques

Finally, it behooves (mostly)institutions to check out the broad and increasing range of mathematical methods, ranging from statistical techniques (time series analysis, statistical testing methods) to modeling approaches (physics, inventory, FIFO, and other management science methods).

Good Luck!

REFERENCES

Articles

1. Barnes, Robert M. "A Statistical Method For Setting Stops In Stock Trading", Aug 1970, Operations Research, vol 15, No. 4
2. Cowles, Alfred 3rd, "Can Stock Market Forecasters Forecast?", Econometrica, vol 1,pp. 309-334, 1933.
3. Zweig, Jason "The cost of Investing With The Upper Crust", Wall Street Journal, Saturday, June 20, 2020

Books

1. Bensdorp, Laurens, Automated Stock Trading Systems, Lioncrest Pub, 2020
2. Bodek, Haim, The Problem of HFT, Decimus Capital Markets, E-published 2012
3. Bombardia, Troy Buy and Wait, E-published 2018
4. Bonner, William and Wiggins, Addison Empire of Debt, John Wiley, 2006
5. Cootner, Paul H. The Random Character of Stock Market Prices, MIT Press, Cambridge, MA 1964
6. Encyclopedia of Stock Market Techniques, investors Intelligence, inc. Larchmont N.Y. 1965
7. Galbraith, John Kenneth, The Affluent Society, Riverside Press, 1958
8. Galbraith, John Kenneth, The Great Crash 1929, Mariner Books, 1997
9. Graham, Benjamin, and Dodd, David, Security Analysis(6th Ed.), McGraw-Hill, New York 2009
10. Kaufman, P. J. Commodity Trading Systems and Methods, Wiley, 1978
11. Kindleberger, Charles, and Aliber, Robert Mania, Panics and Crashes, John Wiley, 2005
12. Makay, Charles, Extraordinary Popular Delusions, Dover Publications, 2003
13. Mandelbrot, Benoit, The (Mis)Behavior of Markets, Basic (Perseus) Books, 2004
14. Merrill, Authur Behavior of Prices On WallStreet, Analysis Press, Chappaqua, New York, 1966
15. Pardo, Robert Design, Testing and Optimization of Trading Systems, Wiley, New York,1992
16. Standard & Poor's 500 Guide (2012 Ed.), McGraw-Hill, New York, 2012
17. Tulchinsky, Igor Finding Alpha, Wiley, New York, 2015

INDEX

APPENDIX

Table 4 MicroTrends 1915-2020 Monthly DJIA Prices

MacroTrends Data Download
Dow Jones - DJIA - 100 Year Historical Chart
Note: Real datasets are adjusted for inflation using the headline Consumer Price Index (CPI) with the current month as the base.

Disclaimer and Terms of Use: Historical data is provided 'as is' and solely for informational purposes, not for trading purposes or advice.

MacroTrends LLC expressly disclaims the accuracy, adequacy, or completeness of any data and shall not be liable for any errors, omissions or other defects in, delays or interruptions in such data, or for any actions taken in reliance thereon. Neither MacroTrends LLC nor any of our information providers will be liable for any damages relating to your use of the data provided.

```
series_id,date,real,nominal
DJIA,1915-01-01,1444.94,56.540
DJIA,1915-02-01,1420.18,55.020
DJIA,1915-03-01,1585.96,60.830
DJIA,1915-04-01,1852.79,71.780
DJIA,1915-05-01,1661.40,65.010
DJIA,1915-06-01,1790.45,70.060
DJIA,1915-07-01,1930.24,75.530
DJIA,1915-08-01,2075.15,81.200
DJIA,1915-09-01,2314.86,90.580
DJIA,1915-10-01,2412.58,95.340
DJIA,1915-11-01,2423.55,96.710
DJIA,1915-12-01,2484.70,99.150
DJIA,1916-01-01,2248.11,90.580
DJIA,1916-02-01,2259.27,91.030
DJIA,1916-03-01,2292.27,93.250
DJIA,1916-04-01,2182.98,89.650
DJIA,1916-05-01,2214.49,91.800
DJIA,1916-06-01,2140.96,89.580
DJIA,1916-07-01,2133.08,89.250
```

DJIA,1916-08-01,2184.48,92.250
DJIA,1916-09-01,2412.14,103.730
DJIA,1916-10-01,2389.50,104.610
DJIA,1916-11-01,2378.50,105.970
DJIA,1916-12-01,2113.85,95.000
DJIA,1917-01-01,2105.28,95.430
DJIA,1917-02-01,1969.46,91.560
DJIA,1917-03-01,2080.45,96.720
DJIA,1917-04-01,1909.82,93.230
DJIA,1917-05-01,1963.67,97.380
DJIA,1917-06-01,1893.77,95.380
DJIA,1917-07-01,1850.14,91.750
DJIA,1917-08-01,1655.91,83.400
DJIA,1917-09-01,1619.71,83.460
DJIA,1917-10-01,1424.44,74.500
DJIA,1917-11-01,1389.07,72.650
DJIA,1917-12-01,1401.39,74.380
DJIA,1918-01-01,1471.27,79.800
DJIA,1918-02-01,1471.62,80.390
DJIA,1918-03-01,1408.77,76.410
DJIA,1918-04-01,1408.90,77.510
DJIA,1918-05-01,1389.90,78.080
DJIA,1918-06-01,1450.02,82.580
DJIA,1918-07-01,1388.55,81.230
DJIA,1918-08-01,1382.11,82.460
DJIA,1918-09-01,1392.14,84.680
DJIA,1918-10-01,1379.45,85.510
DJIA,1918-11-01,1281.53,80.930
DJIA,1918-12-01,1285.85,82.200
DJIA,1919-01-01,1260.98,80.610
DJIA,1919-02-01,1351.28,84.810
DJIA,1919-03-01,1398.41,88.850
DJIA,1919-04-01,1435.55,92.880
DJIA,1919-05-01,1611.30,105.500
DJIA,1919-06-01,1633.91,106.980
DJIA,1919-07-01,1589.61,107.160
DJIA,1919-08-01,1527.57,104.750
DJIA,1919-09-01,1615.70,111.420
DJIA,1919-10-01,1695.80,118.920
DJIA,1919-11-01,1447.10,103.720
DJIA,1919-12-01,1464.44,107.230
DJIA,1920-01-01,1393.70,104.210
DJIA,1920-02-01,1206.95,91.180

DJIA,1920-03-01,1347.02,102.810
DJIA,1920-04-01,1189.36,93.540
DJIA,1920-05-01,1150.38,91.810
DJIA,1920-06-01,1120.89,90.760
DJIA,1920-07-01,1077.72,86.850
DJIA,1920-08-01,1095.52,86.160
DJIA,1920-09-01,1070.55,82.950
DJIA,1920-10-01,1103.57,85.080
DJIA,1920-11-01,991.26,76.040
DJIA,1920-12-01,957.29,71.950
DJIA,1921-01-01,1034.23,76.130
DJIA,1921-02-01,1051.82,74.980
DJIA,1921-03-01,1068.59,75.760
DJIA,1921-04-01,1120.41,78.570
DJIA,1921-05-01,1070.98,73.440
DJIA,1921-06-01,1003.89,68.450
DJIA,1921-07-01,997.04,68.370
DJIA,1921-08-01,978.67,67.110
DJIA,1921-09-01,1048.36,71.080
DJIA,1921-10-01,1079.77,73.210
DJIA,1921-11-01,1146.67,77.300
DJIA,1921-12-01,1205.54,80.800
DJIA,1922-01-01,1241.69,81.300
DJIA,1922-02-01,1305.23,85.460
DJIA,1922-03-01,1376.36,89.050
DJIA,1922-04-01,1420.87,91.930
DJIA,1922-05-01,1484.24,96.030
DJIA,1922-06-01,1436.33,92.930
DJIA,1922-07-01,1491.08,97.050
DJIA,1922-08-01,1567.03,100.780
DJIA,1922-09-01,1510.12,97.120
DJIA,1922-10-01,1485.48,96.110
DJIA,1922-11-01,1454.20,94.650
DJIA,1922-12-01,1499.35,98.170
DJIA,1923-01-01,1496.91,97.430
DJIA,1923-02-01,1596.32,103.900
DJIA,1923-03-01,1578.96,102.770
DJIA,1923-04-01,1502.56,98.380
DJIA,1923-05-01,1489.58,97.530
DJIA,1923-06-01,1342.18,88.400
DJIA,1923-07-01,1304.26,86.910
DJIA,1923-08-01,1410.69,93.460
DJIA,1923-09-01,1320.17,87.970

DJIA,1923-10-01,1320.87,88.530
DJIA,1923-11-01,1377.71,92.340
DJIA,1923-12-01,1425.16,95.520
DJIA,1924-01-01,1501.85,100.660
DJIA,1924-02-01,1466.03,97.690
DJIA,1924-03-01,1392.87,92.280
DJIA,1924-04-01,1376.04,90.630
DJIA,1924-05-01,1364.95,89.900
DJIA,1924-06-01,1463.19,96.370
DJIA,1924-07-01,1541.70,102.140
DJIA,1924-08-01,1581.16,104.140
DJIA,1924-09-01,1557.10,103.160
DJIA,1924-10-01,1561.63,104.060
DJIA,1924-11-01,1667.28,111.100
DJIA,1924-12-01,1798.01,120.510
DJIA,1925-01-01,1842.47,123.490
DJIA,1925-02-01,1834.46,122.240
DJIA,1925-03-01,1741.91,116.750
DJIA,1925-04-01,1800.99,120.010
DJIA,1925-05-01,1938.85,129.950
DJIA,1925-06-01,1932.27,131.010
DJIA,1925-07-01,1951.35,133.810
DJIA,1925-08-01,2058.83,141.180
DJIA,1925-09-01,2092.08,143.460
DJIA,1925-10-01,2269.84,155.650
DJIA,1925-11-01,2166.49,151.080
DJIA,1925-12-01,2178.57,151.080
DJIA,1926-01-01,2268.99,157.350
DJIA,1926-02-01,2230.49,154.680
DJIA,1926-03-01,2036.81,140.460
DJIA,1926-04-01,2072.30,143.710
DJIA,1926-05-01,2079.88,143.430
DJIA,1926-06-01,2231.78,153.040
DJIA,1926-07-01,2362.49,160.180
DJIA,1926-08-01,2410.67,162.510
DJIA,1926-09-01,2333.14,158.190
DJIA,1926-10-01,2211.05,150.760
DJIA,1926-11-01,2282.97,156.550
DJIA,1926-12-01,2292.45,157.200
DJIA,1927-01-01,2306.89,156.410
DJIA,1927-02-01,2402.51,161.960
DJIA,1927-03-01,2388.39,160.080
DJIA,1927-04-01,2456.43,164.640

DJIA,1927-05-01,2565.69,172.960
DJIA,1927-06-01,2437.93,166.230
DJIA,1927-07-01,2706.49,181.400
DJIA,1927-08-01,2848.18,189.790
DJIA,1927-09-01,2948.04,197.590
DJIA,1927-10-01,2695.78,181.730
DJIA,1927-11-01,2957.29,198.210
DJIA,1927-12-01,2994.44,200.700
DJIA,1928-01-01,2962.96,198.590
DJIA,1928-02-01,2940.01,194.780
DJIA,1928-03-01,3236.91,214.450
DJIA,1928-04-01,3194.34,211.630
DJIA,1928-05-01,3298.69,219.810
DJIA,1928-06-01,3175.32,210.370
DJIA,1928-07-01,3260.30,216.000
DJIA,1928-08-01,3628.75,240.410
DJIA,1928-09-01,3541.71,237.380
DJIA,1928-10-01,3784.17,252.160
DJIA,1928-11-01,4402.75,293.380
DJIA,1928-12-01,4528.20,300.000
DJIA,1929-01-01,4792.50,317.510
DJIA,1929-02-01,4790.99,317.410
DJIA,1929-03-01,4689.27,308.850
DJIA,1929-04-01,4876.52,319.290
DJIA,1929-05-01,4515.58,297.410
DJIA,1929-06-01,5038.23,333.790
DJIA,1929-07-01,5187.68,347.700
DJIA,1929-08-01,5674.52,380.330
DJIA,1929-09-01,5124.27,343.450
DJIA,1929-10-01,4080.77,273.510
DJIA,1929-11-01,3565.13,238.950
DJIA,1929-12-01,3728.94,248.480
DJIA,1930-01-01,4032.21,267.140
DJIA,1930-02-01,4116.26,271.110
DJIA,1930-03-01,4369.61,286.100
DJIA,1930-04-01,4239.55,279.230
DJIA,1930-05-01,4201.14,275.070
DJIA,1930-06-01,3477.49,226.340
DJIA,1930-07-01,3638.31,233.990
DJIA,1930-08-01,3760.89,240.420
DJIA,1930-09-01,3185.99,204.900
DJIA,1930-10-01,2868.14,183.350
DJIA,1930-11-01,2886.38,183.390

DJIA,1930-12-01,2638.55,164.580
DJIA,1931-01-01,2720.01,167.550
DJIA,1931-02-01,3118.01,189.660
DJIA,1931-03-01,2851.87,172.360
DJIA,1931-04-01,2517.77,151.190
DJIA,1931-05-01,2167.12,128.460
DJIA,1931-06-01,2567.18,150.180
DJIA,1931-07-01,2314.36,135.390
DJIA,1931-08-01,2383.07,139.410
DJIA,1931-09-01,1662.46,96.610
DJIA,1931-10-01,1826.36,105.430
DJIA,1931-11-01,1648.26,93.870
DJIA,1931-12-01,1377.19,77.900
DJIA,1932-01-01,1375.23,76.190
DJIA,1932-02-01,1490.84,81.440
DJIA,1932-03-01,1351.06,73.280
DJIA,1932-04-01,1041.91,56.110
DJIA,1932-05-01,842.95,44.740
DJIA,1932-06-01,813.06,42.840
DJIA,1932-07-01,1029.80,54.260
DJIA,1932-08-01,1398.82,73.160
DJIA,1932-09-01,1378.39,71.560
DJIA,1932-10-01,1201.29,61.900
DJIA,1932-11-01,1101.87,56.350
DJIA,1932-12-01,1180.80,59.930
DJIA,1933-01-01,1218.55,60.900
DJIA,1933-02-01,1044.45,51.390
DJIA,1933-03-01,1134.87,55.400
DJIA,1933-04-01,1590.87,77.660
DJIA,1933-05-01,1804.93,88.110
DJIA,1933-06-01,1994.60,98.140
DJIA,1933-07-01,1788.44,90.770
DJIA,1933-08-01,2002.53,102.410
DJIA,1933-09-01,1854.11,94.820
DJIA,1933-10-01,1723.88,88.160
DJIA,1933-11-01,1919.03,98.140
DJIA,1933-12-01,1953.44,99.900
DJIA,1934-01-01,2096.58,107.220
DJIA,1934-02-01,2007.85,103.460
DJIA,1934-03-01,1976.60,101.850
DJIA,1934-04-01,1950.21,100.490
DJIA,1934-05-01,1824.26,94.000
DJIA,1934-06-01,1843.76,95.720

DJIA,1934-07-01,1696.02,88.050
DJIA,1934-08-01,1788.67,92.860
DJIA,1934-09-01,1758.02,92.630
DJIA,1934-10-01,1785.04,93.360
DJIA,1934-11-01,1968.21,102.940
DJIA,1934-12-01,2004.02,104.040
DJIA,1935-01-01,1929.97,101.690
DJIA,1935-02-01,1928.94,102.380
DJIA,1935-03-01,1899.36,100.810
DJIA,1935-04-01,2047.15,109.450
DJIA,1935-05-01,2069.41,110.640
DJIA,1935-06-01,2227.19,118.210
DJIA,1935-07-01,2378.30,126.230
DJIA,1935-08-01,2409.58,127.890
DJIA,1935-09-01,2485.50,131.920
DJIA,1935-10-01,2632.84,139.740
DJIA,1935-11-01,2662.51,142.350
DJIA,1935-12-01,2695.81,144.130
DJIA,1936-01-01,2796.06,149.490
DJIA,1936-02-01,2845.81,152.150
DJIA,1936-03-01,2945.60,156.340
DJIA,1936-04-01,2744.57,145.670
DJIA,1936-05-01,2875.89,152.640
DJIA,1936-06-01,2949.43,157.690
DJIA,1936-07-01,3061.29,164.860
DJIA,1936-08-01,3065.89,166.290
DJIA,1936-09-01,3094.10,167.820
DJIA,1936-10-01,3266.85,177.190
DJIA,1936-11-01,3378.03,183.220
DJIA,1936-12-01,3316.82,179.900
DJIA,1937-01-01,3400.16,185.740
DJIA,1937-02-01,3428.71,187.300
DJIA,1937-03-01,3388.37,186.410
DJIA,1937-04-01,3145.57,174.270
DJIA,1937-05-01,3131.68,174.710
DJIA,1937-06-01,3035.06,169.320
DJIA,1937-07-01,3304.04,185.610
DJIA,1937-08-01,3158.08,177.410
DJIA,1937-09-01,2732.64,154.570
DJIA,1937-10-01,2442.71,138.170
DJIA,1937-11-01,2198.07,123.480
DJIA,1937-12-01,2166.24,120.850
DJIA,1938-01-01,2215.23,121.870

DJIA,1938-02-01,2373.19,129.640
DJIA,1938-03-01,1811.38,98.950
DJIA,1938-04-01,2022.74,111.280
DJIA,1938-05-01,1972.29,107.740
DJIA,1938-06-01,2450.81,133.880
DJIA,1938-07-01,2585.72,141.250
DJIA,1938-08-01,2549.48,139.270
DJIA,1938-09-01,2589.38,141.450
DJIA,1938-10-01,2797.45,151.730
DJIA,1938-11-01,2762.23,149.820
DJIA,1938-12-01,2853.31,154.760
DJIA,1939-01-01,2650.50,143.760
DJIA,1939-02-01,2735.21,147.300
DJIA,1939-03-01,2448.14,131.840
DJIA,1939-04-01,2402.53,128.450
DJIA,1939-05-01,2584.52,138.180
DJIA,1939-06-01,2443.30,130.630
DJIA,1939-07-01,2679.54,143.260
DJIA,1939-08-01,2514.00,134.410
DJIA,1939-09-01,2792.40,152.540
DJIA,1939-10-01,2800.21,151.880
DJIA,1939-11-01,2686.09,145.690
DJIA,1939-12-01,2769.97,150.240
DJIA,1940-01-01,2698.63,145.330
DJIA,1940-02-01,2701.76,146.540
DJIA,1940-03-01,2727.75,147.950
DJIA,1940-04-01,2736.60,148.430
DJIA,1940-05-01,2142.75,116.220
DJIA,1940-06-01,2230.95,121.870
DJIA,1940-07-01,2325.64,126.140
DJIA,1940-08-01,2386.12,129.420
DJIA,1940-09-01,2445.48,132.640
DJIA,1940-10-01,2481.80,134.610
DJIA,1940-11-01,2415.25,131.000
DJIA,1940-12-01,2400.47,131.130
DJIA,1941-01-01,2272.32,124.130
DJIA,1941-02-01,2232.78,121.970
DJIA,1941-03-01,2230.68,122.720
DJIA,1941-04-01,2085.50,115.540
DJIA,1941-05-01,2075.00,115.760
DJIA,1941-06-01,2162.22,123.140
DJIA,1941-07-01,2261.42,128.790
DJIA,1941-08-01,2212.15,127.700

DJIA,1941-09-01,2167.86,126.820
DJIA,1941-10-01,1987.62,117.820
DJIA,1941-11-01,1914.61,114.230
DJIA,1941-12-01,1847.82,110.960
DJIA,1942-01-01,1793.77,109.110
DJIA,1942-02-01,1744.52,106.790
DJIA,1942-03-01,1605.62,99.530
DJIA,1942-04-01,1528.65,95.350
DJIA,1942-05-01,1597.43,100.880
DJIA,1942-06-01,1636.39,103.340
DJIA,1942-07-01,1663.93,105.720
DJIA,1942-08-01,1663.32,106.330
DJIA,1942-09-01,1706.81,109.110
DJIA,1942-10-01,1763.07,114.070
DJIA,1942-11-01,1759.18,114.500
DJIA,1942-12-01,1823.60,119.400
DJIA,1943-01-01,1917.98,125.580
DJIA,1943-02-01,1987.17,130.110
DJIA,1943-03-01,2049.51,136.570
DJIA,1943-04-01,2009.71,135.480
DJIA,1943-05-01,2095.24,142.060
DJIA,1943-06-01,2114.71,143.380
DJIA,1943-07-01,2016.68,135.950
DJIA,1943-08-01,2038.37,136.620
DJIA,1943-09-01,2078.54,140.120
DJIA,1943-10-01,2051.10,138.270
DJIA,1943-11-01,1922.04,129.570
DJIA,1943-12-01,2015.79,135.890
DJIA,1944-01-01,2038.19,137.400
DJIA,1944-02-01,2021.87,136.300
DJIA,1944-03-01,2059.55,138.840
DJIA,1944-04-01,2009.26,136.230
DJIA,1944-05-01,2097.90,142.240
DJIA,1944-06-01,2176.14,148.380
DJIA,1944-07-01,2130.72,146.110
DJIA,1944-08-01,2143.56,146.990
DJIA,1944-09-01,2139.76,146.730
DJIA,1944-10-01,2136.85,146.530
DJIA,1944-11-01,2148.51,147.330
DJIA,1944-12-01,2208.79,152.320
DJIA,1945-01-01,2228.37,153.670
DJIA,1945-02-01,2325.96,160.400
DJIA,1945-03-01,2239.10,154.410

DJIA,1945-04-01,2399.05,165.440
DJIA,1945-05-01,2426.89,168.300
DJIA,1945-06-01,2357.04,165.290
DJIA,1945-07-01,2322.67,162.880
DJIA,1945-08-01,2485.38,174.290
DJIA,1945-09-01,2591.18,181.710
DJIA,1945-10-01,2660.92,186.600
DJIA,1945-11-01,2730.22,191.460
DJIA,1945-12-01,2735.85,192.910
DJIA,1946-01-01,2902.63,204.670
DJIA,1946-02-01,2710.68,190.090
DJIA,1946-03-01,2817.47,199.750
DJIA,1946-04-01,2900.57,206.770
DJIA,1946-05-01,2961.73,212.280
DJIA,1946-06-01,2838.17,205.620
DJIA,1946-07-01,2627.54,201.560
DJIA,1946-08-01,2417.47,189.190
DJIA,1946-09-01,2181.63,172.420
DJIA,1946-10-01,2098.98,169.150
DJIA,1946-11-01,2057.64,169.800
DJIA,1946-12-01,2127.29,177.200
DJIA,1947-01-01,2166.18,180.440
DJIA,1947-02-01,2147.69,178.900
DJIA,1947-03-01,2088.48,177.200
DJIA,1947-04-01,2011.16,170.640
DJIA,1947-05-01,1994.78,169.250
DJIA,1947-06-01,2080.26,177.300
DJIA,1947-07-01,2129.83,183.180
DJIA,1947-08-01,2051.77,178.850
DJIA,1947-09-01,1991.79,177.490
DJIA,1947-10-01,2040.27,181.810
DJIA,1947-11-01,2004.62,179.400
DJIA,1947-12-01,1998.38,181.160
DJIA,1948-01-01,1906.47,175.050
DJIA,1948-02-01,1837.62,167.300
DJIA,1948-03-01,1954.69,177.200
DJIA,1948-04-01,1957.63,180.510
DJIA,1948-05-01,2059.99,190.740
DJIA,1948-06-01,2029.12,189.460
DJIA,1948-07-01,1918.11,181.330
DJIA,1948-08-01,1914.31,181.710
DJIA,1948-09-01,1878.39,178.300
DJIA,1948-10-01,1995.22,188.620

DJIA,1948-11-01,1826.02,171.200
DJIA,1948-12-01,1898.88,177.300
DJIA,1949-01-01,1926.44,179.120
DJIA,1949-02-01,1876.84,173.060
DJIA,1949-03-01,1920.65,177.100
DJIA,1949-04-01,1880.93,174.160
DJIA,1949-05-01,1825.86,168.360
DJIA,1949-06-01,1808.14,167.420
DJIA,1949-07-01,1915.94,175.920
DJIA,1949-08-01,1937.57,178.660
DJIA,1949-09-01,1971.11,182.510
DJIA,1949-10-01,2064.28,189.540
DJIA,1949-11-01,2077.36,191.550
DJIA,1949-12-01,2188.82,200.130
DJIA,1950-01-01,2216.46,201.790
DJIA,1950-02-01,2234.58,203.440
DJIA,1950-03-01,2253.57,206.050
DJIA,1950-04-01,2344.13,214.330
DJIA,1950-05-01,2433.27,223.420
DJIA,1950-06-01,2267.80,209.110
DJIA,1950-07-01,2242.67,209.400
DJIA,1950-08-01,2303.59,216.870
DJIA,1950-09-01,2394.44,226.360
DJIA,1950-10-01,2360.80,225.010
DJIA,1950-11-01,2378.42,227.600
DJIA,1950-12-01,2430.61,235.410
DJIA,1951-01-01,2528.61,248.830
DJIA,1951-02-01,2531.34,252.050
DJIA,1951-03-01,2480.39,247.940
DJIA,1951-04-01,2592.34,259.130
DJIA,1951-05-01,2488.01,249.650
DJIA,1951-06-01,2418.15,242.640
DJIA,1951-07-01,2569.83,257.860
DJIA,1951-08-01,2693.31,270.250
DJIA,1951-09-01,2681.50,271.160
DJIA,1951-10-01,2584.67,262.350
DJIA,1951-11-01,2554.44,261.270
DJIA,1951-12-01,2622.30,269.230
DJIA,1952-01-01,2636.52,270.690
DJIA,1952-02-01,2552.43,260.080
DJIA,1952-03-01,2644.48,269.460
DJIA,1952-04-01,2518.85,257.630
DJIA,1952-05-01,2570.76,262.940

DJIA,1952-06-01,2671.29,274.260
DJIA,1952-07-01,2702.51,279.560
DJIA,1952-08-01,2658.81,275.040
DJIA,1952-09-01,2615.99,270.610
DJIA,1952-10-01,2602.65,269.230
DJIA,1952-11-01,2742.14,283.660
DJIA,1952-12-01,2821.80,291.900
DJIA,1953-01-01,2811.93,289.770
DJIA,1953-02-01,2768.79,284.270
DJIA,1953-03-01,2715.86,279.870
DJIA,1953-04-01,2666.17,274.750
DJIA,1953-05-01,2632.13,272.280
DJIA,1953-06-01,2583.61,268.260
DJIA,1953-07-01,2652.18,275.380
DJIA,1953-08-01,2506.41,261.220
DJIA,1953-09-01,2533.46,264.040
DJIA,1953-10-01,2636.74,275.810
DJIA,1953-11-01,2699.75,281.370
DJIA,1953-12-01,2695.24,280.900
DJIA,1954-01-01,2805.48,292.390
DJIA,1954-02-01,2826.11,294.540
DJIA,1954-03-01,2912.18,303.510
DJIA,1954-04-01,3075.47,319.330
DJIA,1954-05-01,3142.27,327.490
DJIA,1954-06-01,3200.22,333.530
DJIA,1954-07-01,3338.29,347.920
DJIA,1954-08-01,3222.00,335.800
DJIA,1954-09-01,3471.59,360.460
DJIA,1954-10-01,3391.46,352.140
DJIA,1954-11-01,3724.98,386.770
DJIA,1954-12-01,3909.24,404.390
DJIA,1955-01-01,3952.16,408.830
DJIA,1955-02-01,3981.55,411.870
DJIA,1955-03-01,3960.57,409.700
DJIA,1955-04-01,4114.76,425.650
DJIA,1955-05-01,4107.12,424.860
DJIA,1955-06-01,4363.49,451.380
DJIA,1955-07-01,4486.60,465.850
DJIA,1955-08-01,4509.04,468.180
DJIA,1955-09-01,4477.22,466.620
DJIA,1955-10-01,4364.48,454.870
DJIA,1955-11-01,4636.88,483.260
DJIA,1955-12-01,4703.78,488.400

DJIA,1956-01-01,4533.70,470.740
DJIA,1956-02-01,4658.03,483.650
DJIA,1956-03-01,4929.05,511.790
DJIA,1956-04-01,4952.17,516.120
DJIA,1956-05-01,4570.16,478.050
DJIA,1956-06-01,4676.48,492.780
DJIA,1956-07-01,4877.77,517.810
DJIA,1956-08-01,4746.79,502.040
DJIA,1956-09-01,4476.86,475.250
DJIA,1956-10-01,4503.87,479.850
DJIA,1956-11-01,4437.51,472.780
DJIA,1956-12-01,4671.04,499.470
DJIA,1957-01-01,4481.10,479.160
DJIA,1957-02-01,4329.33,464.620
DJIA,1957-03-01,4408.61,474.810
DJIA,1957-04-01,4573.32,494.360
DJIA,1957-05-01,4654.44,504.930
DJIA,1957-06-01,4623.22,503.290
DJIA,1957-07-01,4638.21,508.520
DJIA,1957-08-01,4417.76,484.350
DJIA,1957-09-01,4161.91,456.300
DJIA,1957-10-01,4022.73,441.040
DJIA,1957-11-01,4088.87,449.870
DJIA,1957-12-01,3959.99,435.690
DJIA,1958-01-01,4061.43,450.020
DJIA,1958-02-01,3970.28,439.920
DJIA,1958-03-01,4003.86,446.760
DJIA,1958-04-01,4071.29,455.860
DJIA,1958-05-01,4132.37,462.700
DJIA,1958-06-01,4270.63,478.180
DJIA,1958-07-01,4477.11,502.990
DJIA,1958-08-01,4542.57,508.630
DJIA,1958-09-01,4752.10,532.090
DJIA,1958-10-01,4851.50,543.220
DJIA,1958-11-01,4961.95,557.460
DJIA,1958-12-01,5212.58,583.650
DJIA,1959-01-01,5286.84,593.960
DJIA,1959-02-01,5389.86,603.500
DJIA,1959-03-01,5373.87,601.710
DJIA,1959-04-01,5552.00,623.750
DJIA,1959-05-01,5730.37,643.790
DJIA,1959-06-01,5708.73,643.600
DJIA,1959-07-01,5965.94,674.880

DJIA,1959-08-01,5873.38,664.410
DJIA,1959-09-01,5564.47,631.680
DJIA,1959-10-01,5676.50,646.600
DJIA,1959-11-01,5786.94,659.180
DJIA,1959-12-01,5964.10,679.360
DJIA,1960-01-01,5484.66,622.620
DJIA,1960-02-01,5531.82,630.120
DJIA,1960-03-01,5413.04,616.590
DJIA,1960-04-01,5264.88,601.700
DJIA,1960-05-01,5473.13,625.500
DJIA,1960-06-01,5586.21,640.620
DJIA,1960-07-01,5377.89,616.730
DJIA,1960-08-01,5458.63,625.990
DJIA,1960-09-01,5058.82,580.140
DJIA,1960-10-01,5027.08,580.360
DJIA,1960-11-01,5173.12,597.220
DJIA,1960-12-01,5334.84,615.890
DJIA,1961-01-01,5614.71,648.200
DJIA,1961-02-01,5734.94,662.080
DJIA,1961-03-01,5860.97,676.630
DJIA,1961-04-01,5878.99,678.710
DJIA,1961-05-01,6034.99,696.720
DJIA,1961-06-01,5924.46,683.960
DJIA,1961-07-01,6069.00,705.370
DJIA,1961-08-01,6215.24,719.940
DJIA,1961-09-01,6033.21,701.210
DJIA,1961-10-01,6056.53,703.920
DJIA,1961-11-01,6208.65,721.600
DJIA,1961-12-01,6290.73,731.140
DJIA,1962-01-01,6022.80,700.000
DJIA,1962-02-01,6071.53,708.050
DJIA,1962-03-01,6062.10,706.950
DJIA,1962-04-01,5686.58,665.330
DJIA,1962-05-01,5242.39,613.360
DJIA,1962-06-01,4797.26,561.280
DJIA,1962-07-01,5093.77,597.930
DJIA,1962-08-01,5189.60,609.180
DJIA,1962-09-01,4916.12,578.980
DJIA,1962-10-01,5007.74,589.770
DJIA,1962-11-01,5513.21,649.300
DJIA,1962-12-01,5536.98,652.100
DJIA,1963-01-01,5798.08,682.850
DJIA,1963-02-01,5629.02,662.940

DJIA,1963-03-01,5776.17,682.520
DJIA,1963-04-01,6073.90,717.700
DJIA,1963-05-01,6152.26,726.960
DJIA,1963-06-01,5962.53,706.880
DJIA,1963-07-01,5847.18,695.430
DJIA,1963-08-01,6132.12,729.320
DJIA,1963-09-01,6161.30,732.790
DJIA,1963-10-01,6328.83,755.230
DJIA,1963-11-01,6289.36,750.520
DJIA,1963-12-01,6372.92,762.950
DJIA,1964-01-01,6559.95,785.340
DJIA,1964-02-01,6683.57,800.140
DJIA,1964-03-01,6793.41,813.290
DJIA,1964-04-01,6772.36,810.770
DJIA,1964-05-01,6854.14,820.560
DJIA,1964-06-01,6923.07,831.500
DJIA,1964-07-01,6981.13,841.100
DJIA,1964-08-01,6981.18,838.480
DJIA,1964-09-01,7265.57,875.370
DJIA,1964-10-01,7246.56,873.080
DJIA,1964-11-01,7242.43,875.430
DJIA,1964-12-01,7231.68,874.130
DJIA,1965-01-01,7469.36,902.860
DJIA,1965-02-01,7474.49,903.480
DJIA,1965-03-01,7331.11,889.050
DJIA,1965-04-01,7581.39,922.310
DJIA,1965-05-01,7546.29,918.040
DJIA,1965-06-01,7090.07,868.030
DJIA,1965-07-01,7202.05,881.740
DJIA,1965-08-01,7294.84,893.100
DJIA,1965-09-01,7600.98,930.580
DJIA,1965-10-01,7823.00,960.820
DJIA,1965-11-01,7708.11,946.710
DJIA,1965-12-01,7867.48,969.260
DJIA,1966-01-01,7983.15,983.510
DJIA,1966-02-01,7677.94,951.890
DJIA,1966-03-01,7436.08,924.770
DJIA,1966-04-01,7461.04,933.680
DJIA,1966-05-01,7064.60,884.070
DJIA,1966-06-01,6932.09,870.100
DJIA,1966-07-01,6729.89,847.380
DJIA,1966-08-01,6222.92,788.410
DJIA,1966-09-01,6110.92,774.220

DJIA,1966-10-01,6331.46,807.070
DJIA,1966-11-01,6210.02,791.590
DJIA,1966-12-01,6163.74,785.690
DJIA,1967-01-01,6667.39,849.890
DJIA,1967-02-01,6584.86,839.370
DJIA,1967-03-01,6773.70,865.980
DJIA,1967-04-01,6995.20,897.050
DJIA,1967-05-01,6628.65,852.560
DJIA,1967-06-01,6667.88,860.260
DJIA,1967-07-01,6987.97,904.240
DJIA,1967-08-01,6944.44,901.290
DJIA,1967-09-01,7118.60,926.660
DJIA,1967-10-01,6737.93,879.740
DJIA,1967-11-01,6688.56,875.810
DJIA,1967-12-01,6891.51,905.110
DJIA,1968-01-01,6475.05,855.470
DJIA,1968-02-01,6343.25,840.500
DJIA,1968-03-01,6326.04,840.670
DJIA,1968-04-01,6844.39,912.220
DJIA,1968-05-01,6726.32,899.000
DJIA,1968-06-01,6677.84,897.800
DJIA,1968-07-01,6530.67,883.000
DJIA,1968-08-01,6608.07,896.010
DJIA,1968-09-01,6881.80,935.790
DJIA,1968-10-01,6963.88,952.390
DJIA,1968-11-01,7182.22,985.080
DJIA,1968-12-01,6862.01,943.750
DJIA,1969-01-01,6858.86,946.050
DJIA,1969-02-01,6526.56,905.210
DJIA,1969-03-01,6688.68,935.480
DJIA,1969-04-01,6756.73,950.180
DJIA,1969-05-01,6648.24,937.560
DJIA,1969-06-01,6157.74,873.190
DJIA,1969-07-01,5719.71,815.470
DJIA,1969-08-01,5836.96,836.720
DJIA,1969-09-01,5656.67,813.090
DJIA,1969-10-01,5923.45,855.990
DJIA,1969-11-01,5591.06,812.300
DJIA,1969-12-01,5480.06,800.360
DJIA,1970-01-01,5080.44,744.060
DJIA,1970-02-01,5282.17,777.590
DJIA,1970-03-01,5308.10,785.570
DJIA,1970-04-01,4934.61,736.070

DJIA,1970-05-01,4683.84,700.440
DJIA,1970-06-01,4546.84,683.530
DJIA,1970-07-01,4858.41,734.120
DJIA,1970-08-01,5059.99,764.580
DJIA,1970-09-01,5009.08,760.680
DJIA,1970-10-01,4950.00,755.610
DJIA,1970-11-01,5175.88,794.090
DJIA,1970-12-01,5440.40,838.920
DJIA,1971-01-01,5632.22,868.500
DJIA,1971-02-01,5685.15,878.830
DJIA,1971-03-01,5835.90,904.370
DJIA,1971-04-01,6062.04,941.750
DJIA,1971-05-01,5814.52,907.810
DJIA,1971-06-01,5665.87,891.140
DJIA,1971-07-01,5444.16,858.430
DJIA,1971-08-01,5681.19,898.070
DJIA,1971-09-01,5612.36,887.190
DJIA,1971-10-01,5294.93,839.000
DJIA,1971-11-01,5246.59,831.340
DJIA,1971-12-01,5590.46,890.200
DJIA,1972-01-01,5665.63,902.170
DJIA,1972-02-01,5800.81,928.130
DJIA,1972-03-01,5865.26,940.700
DJIA,1972-04-01,5934.94,954.170
DJIA,1972-05-01,5961.27,960.720
DJIA,1972-06-01,5750.70,929.030
DJIA,1972-07-01,5696.40,924.740
DJIA,1972-08-01,5923.08,963.730
DJIA,1972-09-01,5844.50,953.270
DJIA,1972-10-01,5830.58,955.520
DJIA,1972-11-01,6198.86,1018.210
DJIA,1972-12-01,6194.58,1020.020
DJIA,1973-01-01,6053.06,999.020
DJIA,1973-02-01,5746.66,955.070
DJIA,1973-03-01,5668.97,951.010
DJIA,1973-04-01,5454.87,921.430
DJIA,1973-05-01,5300.29,901.410
DJIA,1973-06-01,5207.59,891.710
DJIA,1973-07-01,5398.13,926.400
DJIA,1973-08-01,5079.56,887.570
DJIA,1973-09-01,5408.89,947.100
DJIA,1973-10-01,5414.24,956.580
DJIA,1973-11-01,4623.51,822.250

DJIA,1973-12-01,4753.75,850.860
DJIA,1974-01-01,4738.89,855.550
DJIA,1974-02-01,4706.24,860.530
DJIA,1974-03-01,4572.07,846.680
DJIA,1974-04-01,4499.20,836.750
DJIA,1974-05-01,4260.32,802.170
DJIA,1974-06-01,4227.10,802.410
DJIA,1974-07-01,3957.57,757.430
DJIA,1974-08-01,3502.83,678.580
DJIA,1974-09-01,3100.74,607.870
DJIA,1974-10-01,3361.54,665.520
DJIA,1974-11-01,3100.72,618.660
DJIA,1974-12-01,3064.56,616.240
DJIA,1975-01-01,3486.08,703.690
DJIA,1975-02-01,3633.17,739.050
DJIA,1975-03-01,3762.40,768.150
DJIA,1975-04-01,4007.32,821.340
DJIA,1975-05-01,4038.27,832.290
DJIA,1975-06-01,4233.22,878.990
DJIA,1975-07-01,3959.65,831.510
DJIA,1975-08-01,3970.37,835.340
DJIA,1975-09-01,3752.67,793.880
DJIA,1975-10-01,3931.06,836.040
DJIA,1975-11-01,4017.61,860.670
DJIA,1975-12-01,3964.56,852.410
DJIA,1976-01-01,4527.25,975.280
DJIA,1976-02-01,4499.29,972.610
DJIA,1976-03-01,4614.46,999.450
DJIA,1976-04-01,4586.51,996.850
DJIA,1976-05-01,4454.85,975.230
DJIA,1976-06-01,4556.63,1002.780
DJIA,1976-07-01,4450.57,984.640
DJIA,1976-08-01,4378.91,973.740
DJIA,1976-09-01,4437.04,990.190
DJIA,1976-10-01,4301.66,964.930
DJIA,1976-11-01,4215.13,947.220
DJIA,1976-12-01,4455.62,1004.650
DJIA,1977-01-01,4210.68,954.370
DJIA,1977-02-01,4089.35,936.420
DJIA,1977-03-01,3987.19,919.130
DJIA,1977-04-01,3987.52,926.900
DJIA,1977-05-01,3847.16,898.660
DJIA,1977-06-01,3896.11,916.300

DJIA,1977-07-01,3765.89,890.070
DJIA,1977-08-01,3633.76,861.490
DJIA,1977-09-01,3561.25,847.110
DJIA,1977-10-01,3428.89,818.350
DJIA,1977-11-01,3459.85,829.700
DJIA,1977-12-01,3454.34,831.170
DJIA,1978-01-01,3179.77,769.920
DJIA,1978-02-01,3045.66,742.120
DJIA,1978-03-01,3083.21,757.360
DJIA,1978-04-01,3381.94,837.320
DJIA,1978-05-01,3364.12,840.610
DJIA,1978-06-01,3242.22,818.950
DJIA,1978-07-01,3387.86,862.270
DJIA,1978-08-01,3429.24,876.820
DJIA,1978-09-01,3360.25,865.820
DJIA,1978-10-01,3048.56,792.450
DJIA,1978-11-01,3060.28,799.030
DJIA,1978-12-01,3069.50,805.010
DJIA,1979-01-01,3171.41,839.220
DJIA,1979-02-01,3020.94,808.820
DJIA,1979-03-01,3188.34,862.180
DJIA,1979-04-01,3125.51,854.900
DJIA,1979-05-01,2968.61,822.330
DJIA,1979-06-01,3005.87,841.980
DJIA,1979-07-01,2988.71,846.420
DJIA,1979-08-01,3104.04,887.630
DJIA,1979-09-01,3039.89,878.580
DJIA,1979-10-01,2799.48,815.700
DJIA,1979-11-01,2796.81,822.350
DJIA,1979-12-01,2822.36,838.740
DJIA,1980-01-01,2906.07,875.850
DJIA,1980-02-01,2823.33,863.140
DJIA,1980-03-01,2531.69,785.750
DJIA,1980-04-01,2603.97,817.060
DJIA,1980-05-01,2684.43,850.850
DJIA,1980-06-01,2708.78,867.920
DJIA,1980-07-01,2919.13,935.320
DJIA,1980-08-01,2890.10,932.590
DJIA,1980-09-01,2865.33,932.420
DJIA,1980-10-01,2814.15,924.490
DJIA,1980-11-01,2998.89,993.340
DJIA,1980-12-01,2883.29,963.990
DJIA,1981-01-01,2810.55,947.270

DJIA,1981-02-01,2861.37,974.580
DJIA,1981-03-01,2928.29,1003.870
DJIA,1981-04-01,2890.48,997.750
DJIA,1981-05-01,2850.29,991.750
DJIA,1981-06-01,2783.13,976.880
DJIA,1981-07-01,2683.69,952.340
DJIA,1981-08-01,2464.59,881.470
DJIA,1981-09-01,2353.59,849.980
DJIA,1981-10-01,2356.45,852.550
DJIA,1981-11-01,2449.14,888.980
DJIA,1981-12-01,2402.75,875.000
DJIA,1982-01-01,2384.20,871.100
DJIA,1982-02-01,2248.94,824.390
DJIA,1982-03-01,2246.98,822.770
DJIA,1982-04-01,2307.54,848.360
DJIA,1982-05-01,2207.84,819.540
DJIA,1982-06-01,2160.55,811.930
DJIA,1982-07-01,2140.36,808.600
DJIA,1982-08-01,2381.26,901.310
DJIA,1982-09-01,2363.41,896.250
DJIA,1982-10-01,2606.24,991.720
DJIA,1982-11-01,2737.46,1039.280
DJIA,1982-12-01,2768.10,1046.540
DJIA,1983-01-01,2838.77,1075.700
DJIA,1983-02-01,2933.98,1112.620
DJIA,1983-03-01,2979.89,1130.030
DJIA,1983-04-01,3210.19,1226.200
DJIA,1983-05-01,3122.35,1199.980
DJIA,1983-06-01,3169.76,1221.960
DJIA,1983-07-01,3098.78,1199.220
DJIA,1983-08-01,3132.83,1216.160
DJIA,1983-09-01,3160.51,1233.130
DJIA,1983-10-01,3131.61,1225.200
DJIA,1983-11-01,3255.13,1276.020
DJIA,1983-12-01,3207.01,1258.640
DJIA,1984-01-01,3091.73,1220.580
DJIA,1984-02-01,2910.82,1154.630
DJIA,1984-03-01,2930.86,1164.890
DJIA,1984-04-01,2931.56,1170.750
DJIA,1984-05-01,2757.71,1104.850
DJIA,1984-06-01,2818.54,1132.400
DJIA,1984-07-01,2764.78,1115.280
DJIA,1984-08-01,3024.22,1224.380

DJIA,1984-09-01,2966.09,1206.710
DJIA,1984-10-01,2959.29,1207.380
DJIA,1984-11-01,2914.09,1188.940
DJIA,1984-12-01,2969.56,1211.570
DJIA,1985-01-01,3148.73,1286.770
DJIA,1985-02-01,3126.56,1284.010
DJIA,1985-03-01,3073.21,1266.780
DJIA,1985-04-01,3038.21,1258.060
DJIA,1985-05-01,3164.88,1315.410
DJIA,1985-06-01,3203.77,1335.460
DJIA,1985-07-01,3225.80,1347.450
DJIA,1985-08-01,3188.28,1334.010
DJIA,1985-09-01,3166.13,1328.630
DJIA,1985-10-01,3263.99,1374.310
DJIA,1985-11-01,3486.00,1472.130
DJIA,1985-12-01,3653.23,1546.670
DJIA,1986-01-01,3699.68,1570.990
DJIA,1986-02-01,4036.80,1709.060
DJIA,1986-03-01,4313.74,1818.610
DJIA,1986-04-01,4240.52,1783.980
DJIA,1986-05-01,4447.80,1876.710
DJIA,1986-06-01,4461.14,1892.720
DJIA,1986-07-01,4184.41,1775.310
DJIA,1986-08-01,4466.79,1898.340
DJIA,1986-09-01,4139.67,1767.580
DJIA,1986-10-01,4393.84,1877.710
DJIA,1986-11-01,4475.47,1914.230
DJIA,1986-12-01,4428.94,1895.950
DJIA,1987-01-01,5008.81,2158.040
DJIA,1987-02-01,5144.09,2223.990
DJIA,1987-03-01,5307.70,2304.690
DJIA,1987-04-01,5235.76,2286.360
DJIA,1987-05-01,5229.36,2291.570
DJIA,1987-06-01,5499.74,2418.530
DJIA,1987-07-01,5833.45,2572.070
DJIA,1987-08-01,6007.62,2662.950
DJIA,1987-09-01,5826.05,2596.280
DJIA,1987-10-01,4463.51,1993.530
DJIA,1987-11-01,4101.65,1833.550
DJIA,1987-12-01,4337.16,1938.830
DJIA,1988-01-01,4368.79,1958.220
DJIA,1988-02-01,4609.35,2071.620
DJIA,1988-03-01,4405.54,1988.060

DJIA,1988-04-01,4479.26,2032.330
DJIA,1988-05-01,4462.37,2031.120
DJIA,1988-06-01,4683.92,2141.710
DJIA,1988-07-01,4636.37,2128.730
DJIA,1988-08-01,4406.65,2031.650
DJIA,1988-09-01,4553.32,2112.910
DJIA,1988-10-01,4613.15,2148.650
DJIA,1988-11-01,4537.74,2114.510
DJIA,1988-12-01,4645.08,2168.570
DJIA,1989-01-01,4991.48,2342.320
DJIA,1989-02-01,4794.56,2258.390
DJIA,1989-03-01,4841.83,2293.620
DJIA,1989-04-01,5072.22,2418.800
DJIA,1989-05-01,5171.11,2480.150
DJIA,1989-06-01,5075.32,2440.060
DJIA,1989-07-01,5520.87,2660.660
DJIA,1989-08-01,5671.62,2737.270
DJIA,1989-09-01,5560.67,2692.820
DJIA,1989-10-01,5435.64,2645.080
DJIA,1989-11-01,5547.85,2706.270
DJIA,1989-12-01,5635.80,2753.200
DJIA,1990-01-01,5248.43,2590.540
DJIA,1990-02-01,5299.16,2627.250
DJIA,1990-03-01,5430.66,2707.210
DJIA,1990-04-01,5318.83,2656.760
DJIA,1990-05-01,5747.57,2876.660
DJIA,1990-06-01,5723.93,2880.690
DJIA,1990-07-01,5749.39,2905.200
DJIA,1990-08-01,5126.76,2614.360
DJIA,1990-09-01,4770.07,2452.480
DJIA,1990-10-01,4721.02,2442.330
DJIA,1990-11-01,4937.56,2559.650
DJIA,1990-12-01,5080.33,2633.660
DJIA,1991-01-01,5248.40,2736.390
DJIA,1991-02-01,5519.37,2882.180
DJIA,1991-03-01,5571.30,2913.860
DJIA,1991-04-01,5512.94,2887.870
DJIA,1991-05-01,5764.36,3027.500
DJIA,1991-06-01,5517.01,2906.750
DJIA,1991-07-01,5732.03,3024.820
DJIA,1991-08-01,5752.40,3043.600
DJIA,1991-09-01,5674.54,3016.770
DJIA,1991-10-01,5766.84,3069.100

DJIA,1991-11-01,5421.74,2894.680
DJIA,1991-12-01,5932.05,3168.830
DJIA,1992-01-01,6024.53,3223.400
DJIA,1992-02-01,6084.46,3267.700
DJIA,1992-03-01,5995.38,3235.500
DJIA,1992-04-01,6214.34,3359.100
DJIA,1992-05-01,6277.47,3396.900
DJIA,1992-06-01,6109.36,3318.500
DJIA,1992-07-01,6234.41,3393.800
DJIA,1992-08-01,5967.56,3257.400
DJIA,1992-09-01,5977.40,3271.700
DJIA,1992-10-01,5871.87,3226.300
DJIA,1992-11-01,6008.85,3305.200
DJIA,1992-12-01,6004.72,3301.110
DJIA,1993-01-01,5991.10,3310.000
DJIA,1993-02-01,6080.94,3370.810
DJIA,1993-03-01,6172.89,3435.110
DJIA,1993-04-01,6142.17,3427.550
DJIA,1993-05-01,6314.10,3527.430
DJIA,1993-06-01,6286.75,3516.080
DJIA,1993-07-01,6328.57,3539.470
DJIA,1993-08-01,6510.18,3651.250
DJIA,1993-09-01,6324.56,3555.120
DJIA,1993-10-01,6522.01,3680.590
DJIA,1993-11-01,6520.59,3683.950
DJIA,1993-12-01,6644.74,3754.090
DJIA,1994-01-01,7021.81,3978.360
DJIA,1994-02-01,6740.52,3832.020
DJIA,1994-03-01,6373.84,3635.960
DJIA,1994-04-01,6446.64,3681.690
DJIA,1994-05-01,6577.15,3758.370
DJIA,1994-06-01,6321.93,3624.960
DJIA,1994-07-01,6546.47,3764.500
DJIA,1994-08-01,6778.04,3913.420
DJIA,1994-09-01,6641.03,3843.190
DJIA,1994-10-01,6749.32,3908.120
DJIA,1994-11-01,6446.43,3739.230
DJIA,1994-12-01,6610.57,3834.440
DJIA,1995-01-01,6599.91,3843.860
DJIA,1995-02-01,6862.91,4011.050
DJIA,1995-03-01,7088.86,4157.690
DJIA,1995-04-01,7341.84,4321.270
DJIA,1995-05-01,7572.88,4465.140

DJIA,1995-06-01,7713.48,4556.100
DJIA,1995-07-01,7971.44,4708.470
DJIA,1995-08-01,7782.63,4610.560
DJIA,1995-09-01,8069.60,4789.080
DJIA,1995-10-01,7984.45,4755.480
DJIA,1995-11-01,8525.14,5074.490
DJIA,1995-12-01,8607.00,5117.120
DJIA,1996-01-01,9020.94,5395.300
DJIA,1996-02-01,9139.04,5485.620
DJIA,1996-03-01,9263.48,5587.140
DJIA,1996-04-01,9194.55,5569.080
DJIA,1996-05-01,9299.96,5643.180
DJIA,1996-06-01,9313.18,5654.630
DJIA,1996-07-01,9089.53,5528.910
DJIA,1996-08-01,9216.20,5616.210
DJIA,1996-09-01,9623.23,5882.170
DJIA,1996-10-01,9833.92,6029.380
DJIA,1996-11-01,10610.81,6521.700
DJIA,1996-12-01,10491.34,6448.270
DJIA,1997-01-01,11050.83,6813.090
DJIA,1997-02-01,11121.31,6877.740
DJIA,1997-03-01,10619.15,6583.480
DJIA,1997-04-01,11291.50,7009.000
DJIA,1997-05-01,11817.57,7331.000
DJIA,1997-06-01,12353.21,7672.800
DJIA,1997-07-01,13221.94,8222.600
DJIA,1997-08-01,12233.95,7622.400
DJIA,1997-09-01,12720.43,7945.300
DJIA,1997-10-01,11885.03,7442.100
DJIA,1997-11-01,12501.31,7823.100
DJIA,1997-12-01,12653.28,7908.300
DJIA,1998-01-01,12626.68,7906.500
DJIA,1998-02-01,13621.88,8545.720
DJIA,1998-03-01,14000.50,8799.810
DJIA,1998-04-01,14392.63,9063.370
DJIA,1998-05-01,14106.42,8899.950
DJIA,1998-06-01,14180.00,8952.020
DJIA,1998-07-01,14053.36,8883.290
DJIA,1998-08-01,11911.73,7539.070
DJIA,1998-09-01,12375.65,7842.620
DJIA,1998-10-01,13523.97,8592.100
DJIA,1998-11-01,14349.45,9116.550
DJIA,1998-12-01,14460.75,9181.430

```
DJIA,1999-01-01,14702.72,9358.830
DJIA,1999-02-01,14602.02,9306.580
DJIA,1999-03-01,15305.55,9786.160
DJIA,1999-04-01,16755.38,10789.040
DJIA,1999-05-01,16399.28,10559.740
DJIA,1999-06-01,17037.65,10970.800
DJIA,1999-07-01,16494.17,10655.150
DJIA,1999-08-01,16731.24,10829.280
DJIA,1999-09-01,15887.89,10336.950
DJIA,1999-10-01,16470.34,10729.860
DJIA,1999-11-01,16686.56,10877.810
DJIA,1999-12-01,17636.58,11497.120
DJIA,2000-01-01,16728.07,10940.530
DJIA,2000-02-01,15395.03,10128.310
DJIA,2000-03-01,16470.26,10921.920
DJIA,2000-04-01,16176.00,10733.910
DJIA,2000-05-01,15836.11,10522.330
DJIA,2000-06-01,15640.49,10447.890
DJIA,2000-07-01,15719.84,10521.980
DJIA,2000-08-01,16755.36,11215.100
DJIA,2000-09-01,15827.27,10650.920
DJIA,2000-10-01,16270.20,10971.140
DJIA,2000-11-01,15444.69,10414.490
DJIA,2000-12-01,15998.59,10787.990
DJIA,2001-01-01,16047.97,10887.360
DJIA,2001-02-01,15407.07,10495.280
DJIA,2001-03-01,14472.41,9878.780
DJIA,2001-04-01,15662.32,10734.970
DJIA,2001-05-01,15855.05,10911.940
DJIA,2001-06-01,15228.48,10502.400
DJIA,2001-07-01,15300.17,10522.810
DJIA,2001-08-01,14466.94,9949.750
DJIA,2001-09-01,12811.27,8847.560
DJIA,2001-10-01,13186.18,9075.140
DJIA,2001-11-01,14334.02,9851.560
DJIA,2001-12-01,14641.51,10021.570
DJIA,2002-01-01,14453.44,9920.000
DJIA,2002-02-01,14674.10,10106.130
DJIA,2002-03-01,15023.29,10403.940
DJIA,2002-04-01,14282.77,9946.220
DJIA,2002-05-01,14252.66,9925.250
DJIA,2002-06-01,13264.08,9243.260
DJIA,2002-07-01,12519.53,8736.590
```

DJIA,2002-08-01,12371.48,8663.500
DJIA,2002-09-01,10826.09,7591.930
DJIA,2002-10-01,11957.37,8397.030
DJIA,2002-11-01,12668.03,8896.090
DJIA,2002-12-01,11903.51,8341.630
DJIA,2003-01-01,11444.46,8053.810
DJIA,2003-02-01,11126.42,7891.080
DJIA,2003-03-01,11196.97,7992.130
DJIA,2003-04-01,11906.05,8480.090
DJIA,2003-05-01,12452.32,8850.260
DJIA,2003-06-01,12624.54,8985.440
DJIA,2003-07-01,12964.26,9233.800
DJIA,2003-08-01,13163.32,9415.820
DJIA,2003-09-01,12929.43,9275.060
DJIA,2003-10-01,13672.56,9801.120
DJIA,2003-11-01,13685.66,9782.460
DJIA,2003-12-01,14645.94,10453.920
DJIA,2004-01-01,14620.37,10488.070
DJIA,2004-02-01,14669.31,10583.920
DJIA,2004-03-01,14262.55,10357.700
DJIA,2004-04-01,14039.71,10225.570
DJIA,2004-05-01,13907.23,10188.450
DJIA,2004-06-01,14202.69,10435.480
DJIA,2004-07-01,13820.42,10139.710
DJIA,2004-08-01,13856.88,10173.920
DJIA,2004-09-01,13699.09,10080.270
DJIA,2004-10-01,13557.14,10027.470
DJIA,2004-11-01,14088.26,10428.020
DJIA,2004-12-01,14621.76,10783.010
DJIA,2005-01-01,14203.38,10489.940
DJIA,2005-02-01,14491.35,10766.230
DJIA,2005-03-01,14022.52,10503.760
DJIA,2005-04-01,13515.27,10192.510
DJIA,2005-05-01,13900.81,10467.480
DJIA,2005-06-01,13634.89,10274.970
DJIA,2005-07-01,14056.64,10640.910
DJIA,2005-08-01,13772.82,10481.600
DJIA,2005-09-01,13718.17,10568.700
DJIA,2005-10-01,13530.33,10440.070
DJIA,2005-11-01,14112.47,10805.870
DJIA,2005-12-01,14061.36,10717.500
DJIA,2006-01-01,14146.05,10864.860
DJIA,2006-02-01,14280.44,10993.410

DJIA,2006-03-01,14353.24,11109.320
DJIA,2006-04-01,14561.31,11367.140
DJIA,2006-05-01,14239.60,11168.310
DJIA,2006-06-01,14183.08,11150.220
DJIA,2006-07-01,14183.44,11185.680
DJIA,2006-08-01,14408.54,11381.150
DJIA,2006-09-01,14855.78,11679.070
DJIA,2006-10-01,15451.25,12080.730
DJIA,2006-11-01,15656.29,12221.930
DJIA,2006-12-01,15940.37,12463.150
DJIA,2007-01-01,16092.65,12621.690
DJIA,2007-02-01,15556.62,12268.630
DJIA,2007-03-01,15529.42,12354.350
DJIA,2007-04-01,16315.57,13062.910
DJIA,2007-05-01,16911.90,13627.640
DJIA,2007-06-01,16613.28,13408.620
DJIA,2007-07-01,16369.66,13211.990
DJIA,2007-08-01,16576.96,13357.740
DJIA,2007-09-01,17202.79,13895.630
DJIA,2007-10-01,17203.56,13930.010
DJIA,2007-11-01,16420.47,13371.720
DJIA,2007-12-01,16302.46,13264.820
DJIA,2008-01-01,15471.39,12650.360
DJIA,2008-02-01,14952.73,12266.390
DJIA,2008-03-01,14825.83,12262.890
DJIA,2008-04-01,15409.80,12820.130
DJIA,2008-05-01,15052.24,12638.320
DJIA,2008-06-01,13393.01,11350.010
DJIA,2008-07-01,13346.42,11378.020
DJIA,2008-08-01,13598.78,11543.960
DJIA,2008-09-01,12803.78,10850.660
DJIA,2008-10-01,11115.41,9325.010
DJIA,2008-11-01,10727.28,8829.040
DJIA,2008-12-01,10777.41,8776.390
DJIA,2009-01-01,9777.05,8000.860
DJIA,2009-02-01,8588.52,7062.930
DJIA,2009-03-01,9229.62,7608.920
DJIA,2009-04-01,9883.43,8168.120
DJIA,2009-05-01,10259.90,8500.330
DJIA,2009-06-01,10111.06,8447.000
DJIA,2009-07-01,10996.76,9171.610
DJIA,2009-08-01,11357.55,9496.280
DJIA,2009-09-01,11606.17,9712.280

DJIA,2009-10-01,11597.00,9712.730
DJIA,2009-11-01,12341.39,10344.840
DJIA,2009-12-01,12461.52,10428.050
DJIA,2010-01-01,11990.19,10067.330
DJIA,2010-02-01,12297.38,10325.260
DJIA,2010-03-01,12875.96,10856.630
DJIA,2010-04-01,13034.19,11008.610
DJIA,2010-05-01,11991.63,10136.630
DJIA,2010-06-01,11572.44,9774.020
DJIA,2010-07-01,12391.67,10465.940
DJIA,2010-08-01,11837.40,10014.720
DJIA,2010-09-01,12751.48,10788.050
DJIA,2010-10-01,13119.82,11118.490
DJIA,2010-11-01,12987.10,11006.020
DJIA,2010-12-01,13638.31,11577.510
DJIA,2011-01-01,13937.34,11891.930
DJIA,2011-02-01,14255.91,12226.340
DJIA,2011-03-01,14229.29,12319.730
DJIA,2011-04-01,14706.50,12810.540
DJIA,2011-05-01,14354.70,12569.790
DJIA,2011-06-01,14202.00,12414.340
DJIA,2011-07-01,13867.58,12143.240
DJIA,2011-08-01,13227.81,11613.530
DJIA,2011-09-01,12419.43,10913.380
DJIA,2011-10-01,13628.71,11955.010
DJIA,2011-11-01,13744.12,12045.680
DJIA,2011-12-01,13976.89,12217.560
DJIA,2012-01-01,14388.88,12632.910
DJIA,2012-02-01,14687.65,12952.070
DJIA,2012-03-01,14863.55,13212.040
DJIA,2012-04-01,14825.69,13213.630
DJIA,2012-05-01,13917.84,12393.450
DJIA,2012-06-01,14490.10,12880.090
DJIA,2012-07-01,14660.78,13008.680
DJIA,2012-08-01,14661.74,13090.840
DJIA,2012-09-01,14982.40,13437.130
DJIA,2012-10-01,14615.65,13096.460
DJIA,2012-11-01,14601.68,13025.580
DJIA,2012-12-01,14729.05,13104.140
DJIA,2013-01-01,15537.71,13860.580
DJIA,2013-02-01,15628.59,14054.490
DJIA,2013-03-01,16167.60,14578.540
DJIA,2013-04-01,16472.18,14839.800

DJIA,2013-05-01,16748.05,15115.570
DJIA,2013-06-01,16475.11,14909.600
DJIA,2013-07-01,17126.99,15499.540
DJIA,2013-08-01,16350.58,14810.310
DJIA,2013-09-01,16672.90,15129.670
DJIA,2013-10-01,17178.05,15545.750
DJIA,2013-11-01,17807.66,16086.410
DJIA,2013-12-01,18366.94,16576.660
DJIA,2014-01-01,17315.83,15698.850
DJIA,2014-02-01,17937.56,16321.710
DJIA,2014-03-01,17971.76,16457.660
DJIA,2014-04-01,18056.53,16580.840
DJIA,2014-05-01,18138.13,16717.170
DJIA,2014-06-01,18223.21,16826.600
DJIA,2014-07-01,17938.05,16563.300
DJIA,2014-08-01,18551.82,17098.450
DJIA,2014-09-01,18474.50,17042.900
DJIA,2014-10-01,18903.50,17390.520
DJIA,2014-11-01,19486.27,17828.240
DJIA,2014-12-01,19587.55,17823.070
DJIA,2015-01-01,18950.10,17164.950
DJIA,2015-02-01,19945.97,18132.700
DJIA,2015-03-01,19429.30,17776.120
DJIA,2015-04-01,19464.01,17840.520
DJIA,2015-05-01,19541.59,18010.680
DJIA,2015-06-01,19064.31,17619.510
DJIA,2015-07-01,19140.43,17689.860
DJIA,2015-08-01,17899.86,16528.030
DJIA,2015-09-01,17668.90,16284.700
DJIA,2015-10-01,19164.94,17663.540
DJIA,2015-11-01,19279.27,17719.920
DJIA,2015-12-01,19010.71,17425.030
DJIA,2016-01-01,17931.80,16466.300
DJIA,2016-02-01,17986.47,16516.500
DJIA,2016-03-01,19170.64,17685.090
DJIA,2016-04-01,19177.76,17773.640
DJIA,2016-05-01,19103.45,17787.200
DJIA,2016-06-01,19203.02,17929.990
DJIA,2016-07-01,19777.79,18432.240
DJIA,2016-08-01,19725.74,18400.880
DJIA,2016-09-01,19571.41,18308.150
DJIA,2016-10-01,19376.10,18142.420
DJIA,2016-11-01,20443.11,19123.580

DJIA,2016-12-01,21126.22,19762.600
DJIA,2017-01-01,21115.53,19864.090
DJIA,2017-02-01,22060.97,20812.240
DJIA,2017-03-01,21882.35,20663.220
DJIA,2017-04-01,22113.18,20940.510
DJIA,2017-05-01,22164.13,21008.650
DJIA,2017-06-01,22502.51,21349.630
DJIA,2017-07-01,23073.24,21891.120
DJIA,2017-08-01,23067.45,21948.100
DJIA,2017-09-01,23435.72,22405.090
DJIA,2017-10-01,24452.59,23377.240
DJIA,2017-11-01,25388.88,24272.350
DJIA,2017-12-01,25881.02,24719.220
DJIA,2018-01-01,27221.51,26149.390
DJIA,2018-02-01,25955.28,25029.200
DJIA,2018-03-01,24922.62,24103.110
DJIA,2018-04-01,24888.04,24163.150
DJIA,2018-05-01,25050.65,24415.840
DJIA,2018-06-01,24853.92,24271.410
DJIA,2018-07-01,26025.15,25415.190
DJIA,2018-08-01,26587.98,25964.820
DJIA,2018-09-01,27040.39,26458.310
DJIA,2018-10-01,25643.19,25115.760
DJIA,2018-11-01,26151.38,25538.460
DJIA,2018-12-01,23957.30,23327.460
DJIA,2019-01-01,25624.66,24999.670
DJIA,2019-02-01,26460.24,25916.000
DJIA,2019-03-01,26317.61,25928.680
DJIA,2019-04-01,26858.84,26592.910
DJIA,2019-05-01,25013.56,24815.040
DJIA,2019-06-01,26812.76,26599.960
DJIA,2019-07-01,27025.46,26864.270
DJIA,2019-08-01,26561.70,26403.280
DJIA,2019-09-01,27051.41,26916.830
DJIA,2019-10-01,27127.37,27046.230
DJIA,2019-11-01,28163.62,28051.410
DJIA,2019-12-01,28652.59,28538.440
DJIA,2020-01-01,28284.29,28256.030
DJIA,2020-02-01,25358.54,25409.360
DJIA,2020-03-01,21917.16,21917.160
DJIA,2020-04-01,24345.72,24345.720
DJIA,2020-05-01,23723.69,23723.690

Printed in the United States
By Bookmasters